PARTY ON!

10 PESCATARIAN FINGER FOOD FEASTS FROM AROUND THE WORLD

CARRIE SHAPLEY

Copyright © 2024 by Carrie Shapley

All rights reserved. This book may not be reproduced or stored in whole or in part by any means without the written permission of the author except for brief quotations for the purpose of review.

First Edition

ISBN: 978-1-963569-92-6 (hard cover)
      978-1-963569-93-3 (soft cover)

Shapley. Carrie.

Published by Warren Publishing
Charlotte, NC
www.warrenpublishing.net
Printed in the United States

For Dean, my love

INTRODUCTION

Growing up, my family ate fancy finger foods on Christmas Eve, noshing well into the night, with us kids often grabbing one last snack before bed. The menu was always the same, and my mother did all the cooking, with absolutely no help from any of us. I liked the informality of this, and have continued the tradition with my own family. But at my house, the whole family cooks together on Christmas Eve, and our elaborate finger food feast changes year to year.

The annual changes are partly attributable to me loving to try new things, but also to my kids growing up. Their palates and cooking skills developed, and we were all keen for menus to become more adventurous and international. This cookbook grew organically out of that, as I simply love snacking parties. I love eating without silverware; I love the variety and "something for everyone" nature of an hors d'oeuvre buffet; I love the lack of commitment involved in trying a bite-sized morsel; and I love miniaturized food that allows you to boast, "I ate ten of those!"

Over time, I have grown to appreciate other advantages to this type of entertaining. Disparate diets are easily accommodated, as a finger food buffet includes many main-dishy-type items, and menus are easily adapted for carnivores to party with vegans or carb-loading runners to nosh with the gluten intolerant. It is also easy to balance a nutritious menu when you have so many dishes to work with.

It can be difficult to plan this type of party, though, as more dishes to prepare means more moving parts. How do I select a menu? How much food do I need to make? How do I manage my time so everything is ready at once? This cookbook addresses all those questions and takes the guesswork out of planning and preparing. I have mapped out a plan of action for each party, with a list of what to do when, so everything is ready on time. And each chapter is calibrated to a party of a certain size, so you don't have to second-guess quantities. The menus are also balanced nutritionally and flavorfully, so the foods in each chapter harmonize well on a buffet.

As I wrote this book, I had certain guideposts, because I wanted The Average American to be able to follow my recipes and throw these parties. The Average American kitchen has one oven, four burners, and a microwave. The Average American has a full-time job and no catering experience. And most importantly, The Average American lives in a place without access to specialty food markets. So, the whole time I was writing this book, I had two tabs open on my computer: one for my east coast, not-that-great, local grocery store, and the other for my sister's midwestern Meijer's Superstore. If both stores had a particular ingredient, I could use it. If either store didn't, I couldn't. All of which means that when I say you can do this, I really mean it!

WAYS TO USE THIS COOKBOOK:

- Host a nation-themed party with all of the recipes from one chapter.
- Host a nation-themed potluck where each invited household brings one dish made from a recipe in that chapter.
- Cook your way around the world with family or friends who meet and eat together regularly by making all the dishes in a different chapter each time you get together.
- Do a side-by-side tasting of a dish common to many cultures, like meat pies (Brazilian Pastel, Chinese BBQ Char Siu Puffs, Ethiopian Sambusas, Indian Samosas, Mexican Empanadas, Ukrainian Chebureki) or cheese spreads (Ethiopian Cheeze Dip, Mexican Rajas Con Queso Dip, Ukrainian Cheese Dip).
- Host a coffee klatch or afternoon tea with desserts from around the world.
- Make one dish to take to one party as your contribution to a potluck gathering.

HOW THIS COOKBOOK IS ORGANIZED

- Each chapter of this cookbook is organized by recipe difficulty and time to prepare, from least to most. If you are looking for the fastest, easiest recipes, look to the start of each chapter. And if you are looking to show off and/or win a cook-off, best your chances by making one of the two-page recipes from the end of a chapter.
- Each chapter opens with a photo and a list. The photo is a two-page spread of the buffet that you will manifest if you make every recipe in that chapter. The list is a timeline for you to follow if you are making every recipe in that chapter by yourself, flying solo in hosting a spectacular party.

HOW TO MODIFY RECIPES

- This is a pescatarian cookbook (seafood + vegetarian proteins). If you are not a pescatarian, you can certainly substitute meat back in for the meatless vegetarian alternatives specified (cooked, drained ground beef for the veggie soy crumbles; cooked, diced chicken breast for the meatless chik'n; etc.).
- Each chapter is calibrated for a party of a certain size. If you want to cook that chapter for a party of a different size, either double (triple, quadruple …) recipes to feed more people, or cook only part of the dishes in that chapter in order to feed fewer people.

Pizza ai Frutti di Mare, recipe on page 111

CONTENTS

BRAZIL party for 12 8
  Spicy-Sweet Roasted Brazil Nuts 11
  Brazilian Pineapple 12
  Shrimp and Sausage Skewers 13
  "Ham" and Cheese Toasties 14
  Fish Skewers 15
  Brigadeiro 16
  Quibe "Meat" Skewers 17
  Pão De Queijo (Cheese Bread) 18
  Pastel ("Meat" Pies) 19

The recipes in each chapter are organized from easiest and fastest to hardest and longest.

CHINA party for 30 20
  Smoked Salmon Spring Rolls 23
  Almond Cookies 24
  Crab Rangoon Dip 25
  Bang Bang Tofu 26
  Shrimp Balls 27
  "Meat" Balls in Hoisin Sauce 28
  BBQ Char Siu Puffs 29
  Sweet-and-Sour Sauce #1 30
  Sweet-and-Sour Sauce #2 30
  Hot Mustard Sauce 30
  Steamed Dumplings 31
  Vegetable Tempura 32
  Fried Rice Balls 34

Spanakopita, recipe on page 84

ETHIOPIA vegan party for 24 36
- Pineapple Sticks with Dip 39
- Buticha (Hummus) with Fresh Veggies 40
- Cheeze Dip.................................41
- "Doro" Wat Bites..........................42
- Vegan Peanut Butter Cookies 43
- Himbasha Bread 44
- Awaze Tofu.................................45
- "Meat"Balls in Coconut Sauce 46
- Berbere Seasoning 47
- Kolo Snack Mix.............................48
- Injera Dumplings...........................50
- Lentil Sambusa 52

FRANCE party for 30 54
- Shrimp Provençal...........................57
- Cheese Plate with Socca 58
- French Onion Dip with Fresh Vegetables 59
- Chocolate-Hazelnut Dip with Cookies & Fruit........................... 60
- Sablé Breton Cookies 61
- Stuffed Mushrooms 62
- Salmon Croquettes..........................63
- Crab Quiche Bites 64
- Sausages in Crêpes 65
- Beurre Blanc Deviled Eggs..................66
- Gougères 67
- Cheese Tart 68
- Lobster Thermidors 69

GREECE party for 18 70
- Honey-Lemon Dip with Fruit 73
- Hummus with Fresh Vegetables 74
- Shrimp Souvlaki 75
- Olive Tapenade with Feta...................76
- Mediterranean Tuna Salad Cups..............77
- Baklava Thumbprint Cookies 78
- Cod Fritters with Skordalia................79
- Toum.......................................80
- Skordalia..................................80
- Tzatziki Sauce 80
- Falafel Fritters...........................81
- Moussaka Tarts 82
- Spanakopita (Spinach Pies).................84

INDIA party for 18......................... 86
- Spiced Cashews 89
- Dal Dip with Naan Chips................... 90
- Indian Peanut Dip with Fresh Vegetables........91
- Curried Shrimp............................ 92
- Fish Pakoras (Fritters)....................93
- Apricot Chutney 94
- Mango Cupcakes 95
- Palak Paneer (Cheese Sticks)...............96
- Korma Tofu................................ 98
- Samosas...................................100

The recipes in each chapter are organized from easiest and fastest to hardest and longest.

ITALY party for 12 102
- Veggie Skewers 105
- Lemon-Ricotta Cake 106
- Napoletana Pizza Crust 107
- Pizza al Pesto Genovese 108
- Pizza Margherita 109
- Romana Pizza Crust 110
- Pizza ai Frutti di Mare (Seafood) 111
- Pizza di Patate (Potato) 112
- Pizza Vegetariana 114
- Italian Pizza Sauce 115
- Pizza Boscaiola (Sausage and Peppers) 116
- Siciliana Pizza Crust 117
- Pizza Cinque Formaggi (5-Cheese) 118
- Pizza Pugliese (Onions and Olives) 119

MEXICO party for 24 120
- Spiced Watermelon Skewers 123
- Salsa Verde 124
- Shrimp Salsa 125
- Avocado Dip 126
- Stuffed Jalapeños 127
- Molé Brownies 128
- Rajas Con Queso Dip 129
- Quesadillas 130
- Cilantro Pesto 131
- Chipotle Fish Fritters 132
- Fish Tacos 134
- Taco Seasoning 135
- Empanadas ("Meat" Pies) 136
- Chipotle Aioli 137

The recipes in each chapter are organized from easiest and fastest to hardest and longest.

UKRAINE party for 24 138
- Apple Slices and Honey Dip 141
- Roasted Potatoes 142
- Smoked Salmon on Rye 143
- Seared Tuna with Caviar 144
- Pumpkin Syrnyk (Cheesecakes) 145
- Cheese Dip 146
- Cheesy Crackers 147
- Pickled Mushrooms 148
- Pickled Beet Canapés with Goat Cheese 149
- Polenta with Stuffed Onions 150
- Oladyi with Egg Salad 151
- "Meat"Balls in Vodka Sauce 152
- Chebureki ("Meat" Pies) 154

U.S.A party for 18 156
- Ranch Dip with Fresh Veggies 159
- Honey-Mustard Pecans 160
- PB&J Turnovers 161
- Buffalo Chik'n Dip 162
- Rocky Road 7-Layer Cookies 163
- BLT and C Skewers 164
- Mushroom-Blue Cheese Sliders 165
- Shrimp-Corn Fritters 166
- Potato Balls 167
- Mini Chicago-Style Deep Dish Pizzas 168

Molé Brownies, recipe on page 128

GOING IT ALONE
PARTY PREP COUNTDOWN

WEEKS BEFORE:
- ❏ Make Pão de Queijo dough (cheese bread) and freeze
- ❏ Make Pastel (meat pies) and freeze

A WEEK BEFORE:
- ❏ Make Spicy-Sweet Roasted Brazil Nuts

3 DAYS BEFORE:
- ❏ Make "Ham" and Cheese Toasties

2 DAYS BEFORE:
- ❏ Make marinade for Fish Skewers
- ❏ Mix up Quibe for "Meat" Skewers
- ❏ Make Brigadeiro

1 DAY BEFORE:
- ❏ Make Brazilian Pineapple
- ❏ Prep Shrimp and Sausage Skewers
- ❏ Get Pastel out of freezer to thaw

DAY OF PARTY:
Morning
- ❏ Set up food table and choose platters, bowls, and trays for serving all dishes
- ❏ Get Fish Skewers marinating
- ❏ Get Pão de Queijo dough out of freezer and place on baking sheet

2 Hours Before Party
- ❏ Assemble Fish Skewers

1 Hour Before Party
- ❏ Assemble and bake Quibe "Meat" Skewers
- ❏ Bake Pão de Queijo
- ❏ Cook on grill or under broiler: Fish Skewers, Shrimp and Sausage Skewers
- ❏ Re-heat in oven: "Ham" and Cheese Toasties, Pastel

BRAZIL

PARTY FOR 12

A *world-traveling friend questioned my decision to include Brazilian food as a chapter in this book. "Why not Argentina? Or Korea? Or literally anywhere else?," she exclaimed. "Brazilian food is boring," she added. I countered with, "I have friends from Brazil, and the dishes they make are amazing." My friend was undaunted, asserting that my Brazilian friends must be from a border region where more interesting cuisines sneak into the country. They aren't. And so, gauntlet thrown, I set about creating a menu that is part love letter to my Brazilian friends, and part persuasive essay on the merits of Brazilian food. Grilled meat is a big deal in Brazil, so my menu includes tasty Shrimp and Sausage Skewers, Fish Skewers, and Quibe Meat Skewers. And street food in Sao Paulo is amazing, so I've included irresistible Pão di Queijo (cheese bread) and Pastel (meat pies).*

Possibly in a subconscious nod to how chill my Brazilian friends are, this party menu is incredibly un-stressful to make on your own. If you are not much of a planner, prone to throwing together parties rather last-minute, this is the chapter for you.

SPICY-SWEET ROASTED BRAZIL NUTS

Makes 3 cups

Brazil nuts are native to Brazil, from the Amazon region. They have a distinctive flavor that many people don't care for (including me ….). It took quite a bit of trial-and-error to get the balance just right, but this spicy-sweet coating works with the nuts' distinctive flavor and renders them positively divine. When I finally nailed it, hubby and I couldn't stop "testing" and polished off a whole batch in one day.

Ingredients

Spice Blend:

- 3 Tbsp. brown sugar
- 1 tsp. salt (½ tsp. if using salted nuts)
- ½ tsp. chipotle powder
- ½ tsp. smoked paprika
- ¼ tsp. ground cinnamon
- ¼ tsp. chili powder

Nuts:

- 1 large egg white
- 1 Tbsp. water
- 16 oz. raw Brazil nuts (3 cups) or mixed nuts with Brazil nuts (rub nuts in a tea towel to remove loose skins)

Directions

1. Preheat oven to 300°.
2. In a small bowl or mug, combine all ingredients for spice blend. Stir until no lumps remain.
3. In a medium mixing bowl, beat egg white and water with a whisk until very frothy.
4. Add nuts to egg mixture. Stir until nuts are evenly coated.
5. Add spice blend to nuts. Stir just until nuts are evenly coated in spices.
6. Transfer nuts to a greased baking sheet and spread to an even layer.
7. Bake nuts for 30 minutes, stirring every 10 minutes.
8. Transfer nuts to a serving bowl, separating any that are stuck together. Allow nuts to cool before eating.

MAKE AHEAD:
Spicy-Sweet Roasted Brazil Nuts can be made up to a week before serving. Keep in a tightly covered container at room temperature.

BRAZILIAN PINEAPPLE

Makes 4 cups

I like pineapple, so I may be biased. But truly, this preparation of pineapple is extraordinary, and quite possibly the best pineapple I've ever eaten. Sweet, tangy, gently spiced, with the smallest hit of heat, I had a hard time sharing during my taste-test trials.

Ingredients

- 2 whole ripe pineapples (when ripe, a top leaf will come out easily when tugged)
- 1 cup brown sugar
- 2 tsp. ground cinnamon
- ½ tsp. salt
- ¼ tsp. ground cayenne pepper

Directions

1. Preheat oven to 425°.
2. Cut top and bottom off pineapples (about ½" thick pieces). Peel pineapples, being careful to remove all of the "eyes."
3. Cut each pineapple top-to-bottom in quarters. Remove tough inner core (discard).
4. Cut each quarter into 4 long wedges. Cut each wedge in thirds, making pieces that are about 3" long.
5. In a large mixing bowl, combine sugar, cinnamon, salt, and pepper. Mix well.
6. Add pineapple pieces to bowl. Stir gently until the pineapple is evenly coated in seasonings.
7. Transfer coated pineapple to a large, greased, non-reactive baking sheet (no aluminum). Pineapple should lay in a single layer.
8. Bake pineapple for 30 minutes, until pineapple is tender, sugar is beginning to caramelize, and most of the liquid has evaporated.
9. Immediately transfer pineapple pieces to a serving plate or bowl. Flip pieces over as you do this, so the sticky side is up. If you wait, the caramel will harden and fuse the pineapple to the sheet.
10. Serve pineapple at room temperature or chilled. Refrigerate leftovers.

MAKE AHEAD:
Brazilian Pineapple can be made a day ahead of serving. Keep covered and refrigerated.

SHRIMP AND SAUSAGE SKEWERS

Makes 28 - 32 skewers

These are so simple and so good—the sweetness of the shrimp is a perfect mate for the spice of the chorizo. Super-tasty!

Ingredients

Meat:

- 1 lb. raw extra jumbo shrimp, peeled and deveined
- 12 oz. package veggie chorizo
- 1 Tbsp. olive oil
- 28 -32 bamboo sandwich picks (4" long)

Marinade:

- 2 Tbsp. minced fresh cilantro
- 2 Tbsp. olive oil
- 1 Tbsp. lime juice
- ½ tsp. Sriracha hot pepper sauce
- ½ tsp. salt

Directions

1. In a medium mixing bowl, combine shrimp and all marinade ingredients. Stir until shrimp are coated in seasonings.
2. Count the number of shrimp you have. Slice the veggie chorizo into that many pieces.
3. Place chorizo in a small mixing bowl. Add olive oil and toss to coat pieces.
4. Hold one shrimp so that it curves around one slice of chorizo. Thread this pair onto a skewer so that you pierce the shrimp twice (will become top and bottom of the skewer). Skewer remaining shrimp and chorizo in the same manner.
5. Light a charcoal grill and coat the cooking rack with vegetable oil or non-stick spray. Alternatively, preheat oven broiler to high and move an oven rack to the highest position.
6. When coals are medium-hot, lay the skewers on the cooking rack and pour the remaining marinade over top. Alternatively, lay the skewers on a baking sheet, pour the marinade over top, and place under the broiler.
7. Grill or broil skewers for 5 – 8 minutes total, flipping them over in the middle of cooking. Shrimp will be pink, opaque, and firm when done. Do not overcook or shrimp will become rubbery.
8. Transfer skewers to a platter and serve.

MAKE AHEAD:
Shrimp and Sausage Skewers can be prepared through step #4 the day before cooking and serving. Keep covered and refrigerated.

SEAFOOD

"HAM" AND CHEESE TOASTIES
Makes 24 appetizer sandwiches

Brazilian toasties are essentially grilled ham-and-cheese sandwiches, although a common version of them calls for a dousing of bechamel sauce and a baking of them until they are a hot, sloppy mess. Delicious, I am sure, but impossible to eat with your hands in polite company. My version captures traditional flavors while maintaining true finger food cred.

Ingredients

- 1 french bread baguette (3" wide x 20" long)
- ⅓ cup mayonnaise
- 8 oz. havarti with dill cheese, shredded (2 cups)
- 2 tsp. dried oregano
- two 5 oz. packages veggie ham lunchmeat (24 slices total)

Directions

1. With a sharp, serrated knife, cut the baguette crosswise into thin, ¼" slices. Set the two end pieces aside for another purpose (like toast for breakfast). Pair the remaining slices up for sandwiches.
2. Spread a thin layer of mayonnaise on the top side of the top slice, and the bottom side of the bottom slice of each sandwich. Flip each pair around so the mayo sides face in.
3. Top each pair with two pinches of cheese. Distribute cheese evenly and use it up.
4. Sprinkle oregano lightly over all sandwiches.
5. Top each sandwich with one slice of ham (cut as needed to fit bread and stack pieces).
6. Heat a griddle or large, heavy frying pan over medium heat.
7. When pan is hot, fry sandwiches. Take one sandwich, lift the top slice of bread with its toppings and place it in the frying pan, and then top it with the other slice (mayo sides out). Fry sandwiches for about 3 minutes, until golden brown. Flip over and cook for about 3 minutes more.
8. Transfer toasties to a serving platter and serve hot.

MAKE AHEAD:
"Ham" and Cheese Toasties can be made up to 3 days ahead of serving. Keep covered and refrigerated. Re-heat on a baking sheet in a 300° oven for 10 minutes.

VEGETARIAN

FISH SKEWERS

Makes 20 skewers

Whether grilled or broiled, these fish skewers are tender, flavorful, and incredible. Be sure to use one of the firm-flesh fish listed, or your skewers will come off the grill with just the peppers on them.

Ingredients

Marinade:

- ½ cup coconut milk (4 oz.; shake and stir can to emulsify milk)
- ½ cup coarsely chopped white or yellow onion (½ medium onion)
- 3 Tbsp. fresh cilantro leaves and small stems
- 2 Tbsp. fresh parsley leaves or 1 Tbsp. dried parsley
- 6 large cloves garlic (2 Tbsp.)
- 1 Tbsp. peeled, diced fresh ginger or 1 tsp. ground ginger
- 2 Tbsp. lime juice
- 1 Tbsp. olive oil
- 1 Tbsp. soy sauce
- 1 Tbsp. tomato paste
- ½ tsp. ground coriander
- ½ tsp. salt
- ½ tsp. ground black pepper
- ⅛ tsp. red pepper flakes

Fish:

- 1½ lbs. halibut, swordfish, or mahi mahi filets, skin removed and cut in 1" cubes
- 2 sweet red bell peppers, seeded and cut in 1" pieces
- 20 sandwich picks or 6" bamboo skewers

MAKE AHEAD:
The marinade for Fish Skewers can be made up to two days before use.

Directions

1. **For marinade:** In the container of a blender, place all marinade ingredients. Process on high until smooth.
2. Pour marinade into a one-gallon zip-top bag. Add cubed fish and peppers to bag. Agitate gently to coat everything in marinade.
3. Remove air from bag, seal, and refrigerate for at least 30 minutes, and up to 4 hours.
4. Soak bamboo skewers in water while fish mixture marinates.
5. **To assemble:** Thread 2 cubes of fish and 3 squares of pepper onto each skewer, beginning and ending with a piece of pepper.
6. Light a charcoal grill and coat the cooking rack with vegetable oil or non-stick spray. Alternatively, preheat oven broiler to high and move an oven rack to the highest position.
7. When coals are medium-hot, lay the skewers on the cooking rack and pour the remaining marinade over top. Alternatively, lay the skewers on a baking sheet, pour the marinade over top, and place under the broiler.
8. Cook skewers for 4 minutes and then flip over. Cook 4 minutes more, remove, and serve.

SEAFOOD

BRIGADEIRO
Makes 34 bite-sized treats

These are often called Brazilian truffles, but they are actually more like a brownie caramel. And yes, they are as amazing as "brownie caramel" sounds. A national treasure of Brazil, one bite of a brigadeiro and you will understand why.

Ingredients

Balls:

- 14 oz. can sweetened, condensed milk
- ½ cup Nestle Nesquick chocolate drink powder
- 2 Tbsp. Dutch-processed baking cocoa
- 3 Tbsp. butter
- ¼ tsp. salt

Topping:

- 1 cup chocolate sprinkles (6 oz.)

Serving:

- 34 small candy cups (optional)

MAKE AHEAD:
Brigadeiro can be made up to 2 days ahead of serving. Keep tightly covered and refrigerated.

Directions

1. Lightly grease a 3-cup heatproof bowl or baking dish. Set aside.
2. In a 2-quart saucepan, combine all ingredients for the balls. Place over medium heat.
3. Bring mixture to a boil, stirring almost constantly. Boil for 3 - 5 minutes, stirring constantly. Do not leave mixture alone or it will stick and burn. Mixture will thicken until you stir around the edge of the pan and the mixture stays away from the edge for a second or two. (If you have a candy thermometer, the mixture should reach 224°.)
4. Pour chocolate mixture into prepared dish. Scrape mixture from sides of pan, but do not scrape the bottom of the pan (too crusty). Allow mixture to cool completely (if you are in a hurry, you can stick it in the refrigerator briefly, but if it gets cold, it will be too hard to shape and will need to come back to room temperature).
5. Butter hands lightly and shape chocolate mixture into ½ tablespoon balls. Roll balls in sprinkles to cover outside (sprinkles keep balls from drying out and facilitate easy handling when eating).
6. Place brigadeiro in individual candy cups, if desired, or stack on a serving plate. Serve immediately or cover and refrigerate.

VEGETARIAN

QUIBE "MEAT" SKEWERS
Makes 19

Brazilians love chunks of all varieties of grilled meat, and creating a vegetarian alternative was tricky. I am, therefore, pleased as punch to share my recipe for fantastic Brazilian meat-on-a-stick that has no meat in it. Juicy, meaty, and seasoned just right, these are a favorite of all my taste-testers!

Ingredients

- ½ cup bulgur wheat
- 1 cup boiling water
- 6 oz. meatless ground beef (as for burgers)
- ¾ cup plain bread or cracker crumbs
- ½ cup finely minced white or yellow onion
- 1 Tbsp. finely minced or pressed garlic (3 large cloves)
- 1 Tbsp. minced fresh cilantro
- 1 Tbsp. dried parley
- 1 tsp. salt
- ¼ tsp. ground cinnamon
- ⅛ tsp. ground cayenne pepper
- 1 large egg
- 2 Tbsp. olive oil

Finishing:

- 19 flat bamboo sandwich picks or popsicle sticks
- 1 Tbsp. olive oil or olive oil spray

MAKE AHEAD:
Quibe can be made through step #2 up to 2 days ahead of shaping and cooking. Keep covered and refrigerated.

Directions

1. In a medium mixing bowl, combine bulgur and water. Cover with clingfilm or a plate. Set aside to soak for 60 minutes, until bulgur is tender. Prep other ingredients while bulgur soaks.
2. When bulgur is tender, drain off any excess water. Add remaining ingredients to bowl. Mix with hands until well blended.
3. Preheat oven to 400°.
4. Portion meat mixture into 3-tablespoon-sized balls (a 2 oz. ice cream scoop works great for this). Shape each portion into an oblong meatball, sort of like a short, fat pickle.
5. Place meatpickles on a greased baking sheet. Brush tops with the olive oil or spray.
6. Bake for 20 minutes.
7. Remove from oven and insert a skewer up through the middle of each meatpickle. Transfer quibe to a serving plate and serve hot.

PÃO DE QUEIJO (CHEESE BREAD)
Makes 26 two-inch rolls

This is by far the best gluten-free bread I've ever had. Ironically, it is also the weirdest dough I've ever worked with. I have no idea how this silly putty turns into soft, scrumptious, cheesy rolls, but it magically does. Pão de Queijo are best served fresh from the oven. If you aren't making these for a crowd, portion and freeze the dough, then take out and bake just what you need, as you need it.

Ingredients

- 3 ½ cups tapioca flour (1 lb.)
- 2 tsp. salt
- 1 cup whole milk (or ¾ cup skim milk + ¼ cup heavy cream)
- ½ cup olive oil
- 1 cup grated Parmesan cheese
- 10 oz. round queso fresco cheese, crumbled, or 8 oz. shredded mozzarella cheese (2 cups)
- 2 large eggs

Directions

1. In a large mixing bowl, combine the flour and salt. Mix well.
2. In the microwave or on the stovetop, heat the milk and oil to boiling. Pour hot liquid over flour in bowl and mix. Stir until the spoon can no longer handle it. Then knead with your hands until all the flour is incorporated.
3. Allow dough to cool to room temperature (about 10 minutes).
4. Preheat oven to 425°.
5. Combine cheeses in a small bowl.
6. Add eggs to dough. Mix in with hands until dough is smooth but gluey.
7. With your hands still goopy, add the cheeses and mix in.
8. Scrape the dough off your hands and back into the bowl. Wash hands.
9. Grease a baking sheet. Portion the dough into 1 ½ tablespoon-sized balls with either a greased cookie scoop (1 oz.) or greased hands. Place balls of dough on baking sheet spaced about 2" apart.
10. Place rolls in oven and immediately reduce oven temperature to 350°. Bake for 25 minutes, until rolls are golden brown.
11. Transfer pão de queijo to a serving bowl or platter. Serve warm or at room temperature.

MAKE AHEAD:
Pão De Queijo can be made through step #9 and frozen up to 3 months ahead of baking and serving. Freeze balls of dough on the baking sheet, then pop them off and transfer them to a ziptop freezer bag. To bake, place the frozen balls back on a greased baking sheet, allow to thaw, then bake. Pão De Queijo are best served freshly baked.

VEGETARIAN

PASTEL ("MEAT" PIES)

Makes 24 appetizer-sized pies

These hand-held meat pies are a classic Brazilian street food featuring classically Brazilian ingredients. The combination of meatless chicken, creamy mascarpone cheese, mild hearts of palm, and zingy olives makes them not only authentic, but also authentically delicious.

Ingredients

Dough:

- 2 cups all-purpose flour
- 1 cup whole wheat flour
- 2 tsp. salt
- 1 cup warm water
- 1 Tbsp. vegetable oil
- 2 Tbsp. white wine vinegar

Filling:

- 8 oz. carton mascarpone cheese, at room temperature (1 cup)
- 10 oz. package meatless diced chik'n
- 1 cup finely minced white or yellow onion (1 medium onion)
- 2 tsp. finely minced or pressed garlic (2 large cloves)
- 14 oz. can hearts of palm, drained and diced
- ½ cup sliced or diced kalamata or black olives (2 oz.)
- 2 Tbsp. dried parsley
- ½ tsp. salt
- ¼ tsp. ground black pepper

Frying:

- 2 – 3 cups vegetable oil

Directions

1. **For dough:** In a large mixing bowl, combine flours and salt.
2. Add remaining ingredients for dough. Mix with hands until a smooth dough forms.
3. Cover bowl with a damp towel and let dough rest for 30 minutes. Prepare filling while dough rests.
4. **For filling:** In a separate large mixing bowl, combine all ingredients for filling. Stir until well blended.
5. **To assemble:** Roll dough into a snake and cut into 24 equal pieces.
6. Using a rolling pin, roll one portion of dough out to form a 3" x 5" oval.
7. Top dough with 1 ½ tablespoons filling (a 1 oz. cookie scoop works great for this).
8. Fold dough in half over filling and firmly press edges together.
9. Set pie aside and repeat process with remaining dough and filling.
10. **For frying:** In a large, broad frying pan, heat ½" oil over medium heat.
11. When oil is hot (should feel hot when hand is held 3" above it), add as many pies as will fit in a single layer in the pan. Fry until golden brown (2 – 3 minutes), flip, and fry until browned on second side. Transfer cooked pies to a paper towel-lined plate to blot off excess oil, then move them onto a serving platter.
12. Replenish oil as needed and fry remaining pies. Serve pastel hot.

MAKE AHEAD:
Pastel can be made up to 3 days before serving if refrigerated, and up to 3 months ahead if frozen. Thaw and re-heat on a baking sheet in a 300° oven for 10 minutes.

GOING IT ALONE PARTY PREP COUNTDOWN

WEEKS BEFORE:
- Make Almond Cookies and freeze
- Make "Meat"balls in Hoisin Sauce and freeze
- Make Shrimp Balls and freeze
- Make Fried Rice Balls and freeze
- Make Steamed Dumplings and freeze
- Make Hot Mustard Sauce, Sweet-and-Sour Sauces #1 and #2

4 DAYS BEFORE:
- Bake tofu for Bang Bang Tofu
- Make sauce for Bang Bang Tofu

3 DAYS BEFORE:
- Make Vegetable Tempura

2 DAYS BEFORE:
- Make filling for BBQ Char Siu Puffs
- Make Crab Rangoon Dip

1 DAY BEFORE:
- Make Smoked Salmon Spring Rolls
- Remove from freezer to thaw: Almond Cookies, "Meat"balls and Hoisin Sauce, Shrimp Balls, Fried Rice Balls, Steamed Dumplings

DAY OF PARTY:
Morning
- Set up food table and choose platters, bowls, and trays for serving all dishes

90 Minutes Before Party
- Make BBQ Char Siu Puffs
- Bake Crab Rangoon Dip and make Wonton Chips

45 Minutes Before Party
- Re-heat in oven: Shrimp Balls, Fried Rice Balls, Vegetable Tempura
- Re-heat on stovetop: Vegetarian Steamed Dumplings, "Meat"balls in Hoisin Sauce, Bang Bang Tofu

CHINA

PARTY FOR 30

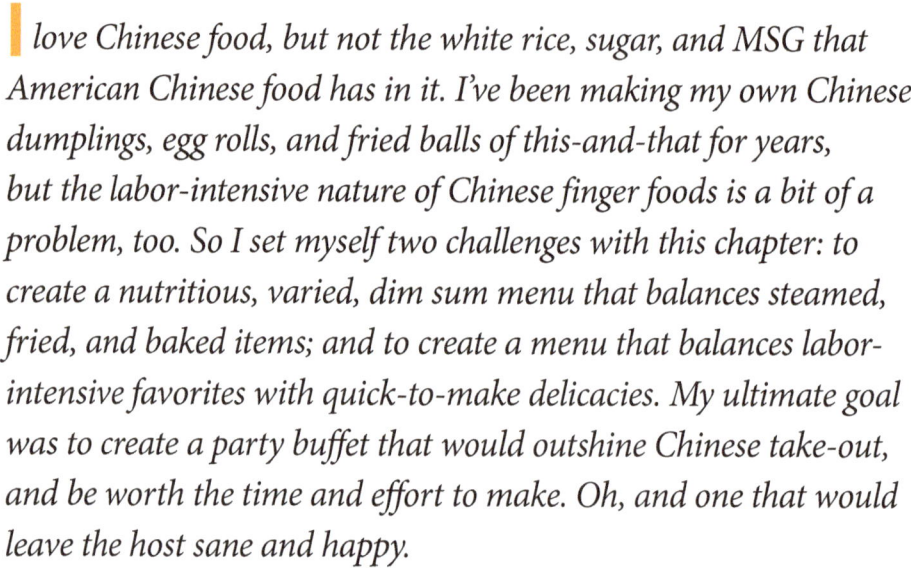

I love Chinese food, but not the white rice, sugar, and MSG that American Chinese food has in it. I've been making my own Chinese dumplings, egg rolls, and fried balls of this-and-that for years, but the labor-intensive nature of Chinese finger foods is a bit of a problem, too. So I set myself two challenges with this chapter: to create a nutritious, varied, dim sum menu that balances steamed, fried, and baked items; and to create a menu that balances labor-intensive favorites with quick-to-make delicacies. My ultimate goal was to create a party buffet that would outshine Chinese take-out, and be worth the time and effort to make. Oh, and one that would leave the host sane and happy.

I believe I have succeeded. To be fair, there are labor-intensive dishes on this menu like the Steamed Dumplings, Shrimp Balls, Fried Rice Balls, and Vegetable Tempura (not hard to make, just time-consuming with all the stuffing, steaming, and frying). But they are balanced by quick-fix dishes like Smoked Salmon Spring Rolls, Crab Rangoon Dip, and Almond Cookies. I hope you will find just the right occasion to make this chapter, as the result will be the most delicious dim sum experience ever to grace your table.

SMOKED SALMON SPRING ROLLS

Makes 12 spring rolls; 24 pieces

This is a great appetizer for summer—easy, colorful, tasty, and no cooking required! Brown rice wrappers are the healthier choice, but I must warn you that they are also a weird brown-ricey color. I hate to say this, as I am all for nutrition, but if you are making these for a party where looks matter, you should opt for the white rice wrappers.

Ingredients

Filling:

- 12 oz. bag coleslaw mix (4 cups shredded green cabbage + 2 cups shredded carrots)
- ¼ cup Sriracha mayo (store-bought or homemade: ¼ cup mayonnaise + ¾ tsp. Sriracha hot sauce)
- two 14 oz. cans sliced bamboo shoots, drained
- 2 tsp. soy sauce
- 1 tsp. sesame oil
- 8 oz. package sliced, cold-smoked nova salmon

Wrappers:

- twelve 8" diameter rice paper spring roll wrappers (4 oz. white or brown rice)
- 1 cup hot (not boiling) water

Directions

1. **For filling:** In a medium mixing bowl, combine coleslaw mix and mayo. Mix until everything is coated in mayo. Set aside.
2. Cut the bamboo shoots into thin sticks. Transfer them to a small mxing bowl.
3. Add soy sauce and sesame oil to the bamboo shoots. Stir until shoots are thoroughly coated. Set aside.
4. Remove salmon from package. Peel slices apart and divide into 12 equal portions.
5. **To assemble:** Pour hot water for the wrappers into a pie plate.
6. Dip one rice paper wrapper into the water. Submerge it and immediately pull it out, letting excess water drip off.
7. Lay the moistened wrapper on a bamboo sushi mat or a lightly oiled dinner plate.
8. Top the wrapper with the filling ingredients, in these quantities and in this order: 1 mounded tablespoon bamboo shoots, then 1 portion salmon, then 2 mounded tablespoons coleslaw. Lay the filling ingredients in a rectangular pile (about 1" x 4 ½"), across the middle of the wrapper.
9. Fold the two ends of the wrapper over the pile of ingredients. Then fold the long side nearest you over the ingredients and roll the wrapper up around ingredients like a burrito. Roll as tightly as you can.
10. Transfer finished spring roll to a cutting surface. With a sharp knife, make a diagonal cut to slice the roll in half.
11. Transfer spring roll pieces to a serving platter. Repeat rolling and cutting process with remaining wrappers and ingredients. Serve immediately.

MAKE AHEAD:

Smoked Salmon Spring Rolls can be made the day before serving. Keep covered and refrigerated. Leave rolls whole and slice in half just before serving.

SEAFOOD

ALMOND COOKIES
Makes 60 two-inch cookies

For Chinese New Year, almond cookies symbolize coins and thus, good fortune. They are a Chinese-American invention, so not entirely "authentic," but they are popular in the U.S., the U.K., and Hong Kong. Most important for me, you won't have to find a specialty market to get the ingredients for them.

Ingredients

Dough:

- 1 cup butter, at room temperature (2 sticks)
- 2 cups granulated sugar
- 4 large eggs
- 2 tsp. almond extract
- 4 cups almond flour
- 2 cups all-purpose flour
- 1 Tbsp. baking powder
- 1 tsp. salt

Topping:

- 60 whole, blanched almonds (4 oz.)
- 1 egg yolk + 2 tsp. water

Directions

1. In a large mixing bowl, cream together butter and sugar.
2. Add eggs and almond extract. Beat with a whisk. Mixture will not be smooth.
3. Add remaining ingredients for dough. Mix with a sturdy spoon or your hands just until no dry bits remain.
4. Preheat oven to 325°.
5. Roll dough into 1 tablespoon-sized balls (a ⅔ oz. cookie scoop works great for this). Place balls on an ungreased baking sheet. Cookies won't spread much, so balls can be placed an inch and a half apart.
6. Flatten balls into thick discs. Top each with an almond, lightly pressed in.
7. In a mug or small bowl, combine yolk and water. Mix well. Brush yolk mixture lightly over cookies.
8. Bake cookies for 12-15 minutes, until just beginning to brown around the edges. Transfer cookies to a cooling rack and allow to cool completely before serving or storing in an airtight container.

MAKE AHEAD:
Almond Cookies can be made up to 5 days before serving if kept tightly covered at room temperature, or up to 3 months ahead if frozen.

CRAB RANGOON DIP

Makes 4 cups dip

I love crab rangoon, but they are fussy and time-consuming to make. This de-constructed dip with fried wonton chips on the side has all the flavor of the traditional dish, but with a fraction of the work.

Ingredients

Dip:

- two 8 oz. blocks cream cheese, at room temperature
- 2 Tbsp. soy sauce
- 1 cup very finely minced red onion or green onions (4 - 6 green onions)
- ½ cup grated Parmesan cheese
- two 6 oz. cans lump crab meat, drained
- 8 oz. package imitation crab meat, diced
- ¼ cup snipped chives, fresh or dried

Wonton Chips:

- 1 - 2 cups vegetable oil
- 16 oz. package wonton wrappers (64 wrappers)

MAKE AHEAD:
Crab Rangoon Dip can be made through step #4 up to two days ahead of baking and serving. Keep covered and refrigerated.

Directions

1. **For dip:** Preheat oven to 350°.
2. In a medium mixing bowl, soften cream cheese and mix with soy sauce.
3. Add remaining dip ingredients to bowl. Mix well.
4. Transfer dip mixture to a baking dish. Top with a few more chives, if desired.
5. Bake dip for 20 - 30 minutes, until bubbly around the edges and hot all the way through. While dip is baking, make wonton chips.
6. **For chips:** In a broad frying pan, heat ¼" of oil over medium heat.
7. Cut the wonton wrappers in half, on the diagonal.
8. When oil is hot, fry the wontons, a few at a time, in a single layer, until light brown. Wontons will cook very quickly (less than a minute) and should be flipped over in the middle of frying so they brown evenly on both sides.
9. Remove cooked wontons from the oil and drain on paper towels.
10. When baked, set the dish of hot dip on a platter. Add a spoon to the dip for scooping. Surround dip with wonton chips.

SEAFOOD

BANG BANG TOFU
Makes 6 cups

Americanized bang bang sauce often starts with a healthy dose of mayonnaise (yuck), which is not particularly Chinese. This tofu dish more closely resembles the Sichuan classic, with a spicy, sweet, tangy sauce.

Ingredients

Tofu:

- three 14 oz. packages extra-firm tofu, drained
- 3 Tbsp. soy sauce or tamari
- 3 Tbsp. sesame oil
- 3 Tbsp. cornstarch

Sauce:

- 3 Tbsp. grated fresh ginger (peel, then grate on a microplane or the finest side of a box grater) or 1 Tbsp. ground ginger
- 2 tsp. finely minced or pressed garlic (2 large cloves)
- 4 Tbsp. brown sugar
- 4 Tbsp. soy sauce
- 3 Tbsp. sesame oil
- 2 Tbsp. Chinese roasted sesame paste or natural peanut butter (no sugar)
- 2 Tbsp. rice wine vinegar
- 2 - 3 tsp. Sriracha hot sauce or Chinese hot sauce (for a mild sauce use ½ tsp.)
- 1 tsp. ground ginger
- ½ cup thinly sliced green onion (2 - 4 onions)

MAKE AHEAD:
This dish can be prepared up to 4 days ahead of serving. Keep the tofu, onions, and sauce separate in covered containers in the refrigerator. Combine and re-heat just before serving.

Directions

1. **For tofu:** Cut each block of tofu horizontally into three 4" x 6" slabs. Lay slabs out flat on several layers of paper towel or a folded tea towel, and top with more paper towels or another tea towel.
2. Place a baking sheet or cutting board on top of the tofu, and weigh it down (cans of food work great). Let sit at least 30 minutes, to press excess moisture out of the tofu.
3. Preheat oven to 400°.
4. Cut tofu slabs into 9 pieces each (3 rows x 3 columns). Transfer pieces to a large mixing bowl. Add soy sauce and oil. Using a rubber spatula, gently stir to coat tofu.
5. Add cornstarch. Gently stir until tofu is coated and no white spots of cornstarch remain. (Don't add the soy sauce, oil, and cornstarch all at once — it will make a gloppy mess.)
7. Transfer tofu to a large, greased baking sheet, laying the cubes in a single layer.
8. Bake tofu for 30 - 45 minutes, flipping pieces over in the middle of baking time (tofu should be lightly browned on both sides). While tofu is baking, prepare sauce.
9. **For sauce:** In a 1-quart saucepan or microwave-safe bowl, combine all sauce ingredients except onions. Warm sauce on the stovetop or in the microwave.
10. When tofu is done baking, transfer pieces to a serving bowl. Top with onions. Pour sauce over all. Serve with fork picks or toothpicks.

SHRIMP BALLS

Makes 40 one-inch balls

I struggle to make shrimp siu mai that look like something other than broken bags of crap. I love the combination of Asian seasonings and shrimp, though, so I wanted an easier, more reliable replacement. Many tests and trials later, these beauties emerged from my deep fryer—moist, succulent, irresistible. And they are so simple—just mix and plop! I say bye-bye fussy dumplings, hello easy shrimp balls!

Ingredients

Batter:

- 2 lbs. raw shrimp, peeled and de-veined
- 2 Tbsp. cornstarch
- 8 oz. can water chestnuts, drained and finely minced
- ½ cup sliced green onions (2 - 3 onions)
- 1 Tbsp. grated fresh ginger (peel, then grate on a microplane or the finest side of a box grater) or 2 tsp. ground ginger
- 2 large egg whites
- 2 Tbsp. soy sauce
- 1 Tbsp. sesame oil
- 1 tsp. rice wine vinegar

Frying:

- 8 cups vegetable oil for deep frying (64 oz.)

Directions

1. **For batter:** Mince the shrimp by either pulsing them in a food processor, or chopping them with a cleaver or large, sharp knife. If using a cleaver/knife, lay a shrimp flat on a cutting board, lay your knife flat on top of it, and bash the knife with your fist to smash the shrimp underneath it. Bash the rest of the shrimp and then mince them (the bashing will save a lot of time).

2. In a medium mixing bowl, combine shrimp and cornstarch. Mix until no white spots of cornstarch remain.

3. Add remaining ingredients for batter. Mix well.

4. **For frying:** In a stockpot, deep frying pan, electric fryer, or wok, heat oil to 350° (a deep-fry thermometer is invaluable). Oil should be at least 3" deep. Line a baking sheet with several layers of paper towels or newspaper, lay a cooling rack upside down on top of paper, and set aside.

5. When oil is up to temperature, drop tablespoon-sized balls of batter into oil (the batter is loose and cannot be shaped, so a cookie scoop is essential if you want round balls). Do not crowd the pot—cook the balls in batches as needed. Cook each batch for 4 - 5 minutes total, flipping them over as needed for even browning.

6. Remove shrimp balls from oil using tongs or a kitchen spider and transfer to the prepared tray to drain.

7. Allow oil to come back up to temperature before adding next batch of balls.

8. Transfer shrimp balls to a bowl or platter and serve.

> **MAKE AHEAD:**
> Shrimp Balls can be made ahead and refrigerated for up to 4 days or frozen for up to 3 months. Thaw and lay out on a baking sheet. Re-heat in a 300° oven for 10 minutes.

SEAFOOD

"MEAT" BALLS IN HOISIN SAUCE

Makes 40 one-and-a-half inch meatballs

The sauce for these meatballs is dark, thick, and really luscious. The consistency of it is perfect for serving on a finger food buffet at a nibbling, mingling party, as the sauce clings to the meatballs and won't land on your carpet.

Ingredients

Meatballs:

- two 16 oz. packages meatless ground beef (as for burgers)
- 8 oz. can water chestnuts, drained and finely minced
- 1 Tbsp. finely minced or pressed garlic (3 large cloves) or 1 ½ tsp. garlic powder
- 1 cup thinly sliced green onions (4 - 6 onions)
- ½ cup plain bread or cracker crumbs
- 1 large egg
- 2 Tbsp. soy sauce
- 1 Tbsp. sesame oil

Sauce:

- 6 oz. can tomato paste
- ½ cup molasses
- ¼ cup soy sauce
- ¼ cup rice wine vinegar
- 1 Tbsp. honey
- 1 tsp. ground ginger
- 1 tsp. Sriracha hot sauce or Chinese hot sauce (adds flavor, not heat; increase to 1 Tbsp. if you want heat in the sauce)

VEGETARIAN

Directions

1. **For meatballs:** Preheat oven to 400°. Grease a baking sheet and set aside.
2. In a large mixing bowl, combine all ingredients for meatballs. Mix with hands until well blended.
3. Form mixture into 1 ½ tablespoon-sized balls (a 1 oz. cookie scoop works great for this) and place on prepared baking sheet, leaving at least ½" space between balls.
4. Bake meatballs for 20 minutes. When done, the meatballs will be firm and lightly browned. While meatballs cook, prepare sauce.
5. **For sauce:** In a 3-quart saucepan, combine all ingredients for sauce. Cover and place pan over medium heat. Bring to a boil, stirring often.
6. Boil sauce for 1 minute. Turn burner off but leave pan in place to stay warm.
7. When meatballs are cooked, add them to the sauce. Stir gently to coat balls.
8. Transfer meatballs to a serving bowl. Serve with fork picks or toothpicks.

> **MAKE AHEAD:**
> "Meat"balls in Hoisin Sauce can be prepared through step #6 and refrigerated for up to 4 days or frozen for up to 3 months. Keep the balls and sauce in separate containers. Combine and re-heat (thaw first if frozen) just before serving.

BBQ CHAR SIU PUFFS

Makes 36 - 40 appetizer-sized pies

These are so good! And your friends will never believe that there is no meat in them. Just the right amount of zesty filling tucked inside crispy puff pastry, these really stand out on a buffet with the other steamed, fried, saucy dishes in this chapter.

Ingredients

Filling:

- 10 oz. package meatless diced chik'n
- 8 oz. package smoked tofu or baked teriyaki tofu, cut in ¼" dice
- 6 oz. can tomato paste
- 2 Tbsp. finely minced or pressed garlic (6 large cloves)
- 1 Tbsp. grated fresh ginger (peel and grate on a microplane or the finest side of a box grater) or 2 tsp. ground ginger
- ½ cup brown sugar
- ½ cup soy sauce
- 2 Tbsp. rice wine vinegar
- 1 Tbsp. sesame oil
- 1 Tbsp. Sriracha hot sauce or Chinese hot sauce (adds a mild kick of heat)
- 1 tsp. ground black pepper

Pastry:

- two 16 oz. boxes frozen puff pastry sheet, thawed and chilled
- 1 large egg
- 1 tsp. milk or water

Directions

1. **For filling:** In a 2-quart saucepan, combine all ingredients for filling.
2. Place pot over medium heat and bring to a boil, stirring occasionally.
3. Remove pan from heat and set aside to cool.
4. **To assemble:** Remove puff pastry from packages and place sheets on a clean, well-floured work surface.
5. Unfold puff pastry. With a rolling pin, gently roll out sheets. If each package contains just one sheet of puff pastry, the sheets should measure 18" x 14" and be cut into 20 squares each (5 columns by 4 rows). If each package contains two sheets of puff pastry, roll each sheet to 11" x 11" and cut into 9 squares each (3 columns by 3 rows).
6. Top each square with a scant tablespoon of filling. Distribute filling evenly and use it all up.
7. Preheat oven to 425°.
8. In a small bowl or mug, combine egg and milk to make an egg wash. Mix vigorously with a fork or small whisk to fully blend egg white, egg yolk, and milk.
9. With a pastry brush, lightly brush egg wash onto the edges of each square of puff pastry.
10. Fold puff pastry squares in half, over filling, forming stuffed triangles.
11. Gently press edges together without pinching pastry flat. Transfer triangles to greased baking sheets.
12. Brush tops of all char siu puffs with the egg wash.
13. Bake for 20–25 minutes, until puffed and golden brown. Transfer char siu puffs to a serving platter and serve hot.

> **MAKE AHEAD:**
> The filling for BBQ Char Siu Puffs can be made through step #3 up to 4 days ahead of assembly and baking. Allow mixture to cool, then store in the refrigerator in an airtight container.

SWEET-AND-SOUR SAUCE #1
Makes 1 cup

Quick and delicious—just my kind of dipping sauce! This is great on dumplings, egg rolls, and generally, all things Chinese.

Ingredients
- ¼ cup soy sauce
- ¼ cup rice wine vinegar
- ¼ cup honey
- ¼ cup ketchup
- 2 Tbsp. tomato paste (½ of a 6 oz. can)

Directions
1. In a small bowl, combine all ingredients.
2. Stir with a fork or whisk until thoroughly blended. Cover and refrigerate until needed. Sweet-and-Sour Sauce will keep for 3 months.

HOT MUSTARD SAUCE
Makes 1 cup

This is my new favorite dipping sauce for fried foods. With a hit of heat from the mustard powder and a hint of sweet from the ketchup, it strikes just the right balance. This doesn't have the sinus-clearing power of traditional Chinese hot mustard, but for me, that's a selling feature!

Ingredients
- ½ cup brown mustard
- ¼ cup ketchup
- 4 tsp. dry mustard powder
- 1 - 4 tsp. prepared horseradish (brands vary)

Directions
1. In a small bowl, combine all ingredients, using the smallest quantity of horseradish.
2. Stir with a fork or whisk until thoroughly blended. Taste, and add more horseradish if needed (if in doubt, add more; when you have added enough, you will be certain).
3. Cover and refrigerate until needed. Hot Mustard Sauce will keep for 3 months.

SWEET-AND-SOUR SAUCE #2
Makes 1 cup

Thick and flavorful, this sweet-and-sour sauce requires a little bit more effort, but results in a decidedly more complex dipper than Sauce #1. Definitely worth the extra minutes!

Ingredients
- 1 Tbsp. sesame oil
- 1 Tbsp. grated fresh ginger (peel, then grate on a microplane or the finest side of a box grater) or 2 tsp. ground ginger
- 2 cloves garlic, finely minced or pressed (2 tsp.)
- ⅓ cup brown sugar
- ¼ cup soy sauce
- ¼ cup rice wine vinegar
- 1 Tbsp. ketchup
- 1 Tbsp. cornstarch
- 1 Tbsp. water

Directions
1. In a 1-quart saucepan, combine all ingredients except cornstarch and water.
2. Cover and place pan over medium-high heat.
3. In a small ramekin or mug, combine the cornstarch and water. Stir well, scraping the bottom to dissolve all of the cornstarch.
4. When mixture in pan comes to a boil, add cornstarch mixture to thicken sauce. Cook one minute, stirring constantly.
5. Remove sauce from heat and allow to cool. Store in a covered container in the refrigerator. Sweet-and-Sour Sauce will keep for 3 months.

STEAMED DUMPLINGS

Makes 50 two-bite dumplings

If you aren't able to find frozen, roasted mushrooms at your local grocery store, you will have to roast them yourself. Get 1 pound of sliced white mushrooms, toss them in 2 tablespoons oil, and spread them out on a greased baking sheet. Roast them in a 400° oven for 20 - 30 minutes. Not difficult, just one more thing you have to do :~)

Ingredients

Filling:

- 8 oz. package plain seitan strips, finely chopped
- 8 oz. package frozen, roasted mushrooms, thawed and finely chopped
- 4 cups thinly sliced green onions (2 - 3 grocery store bunches) or Chinese chives
- 1 Tbsp. grated fresh ginger (peel and grate on a microplane or the finest side of a box grater) or 2 tsp. ground ginger
- 1 Tbsp. garlic, minced and smashed into a paste (3 large cloves)
- 1 Tbsp. cornstarch
- 2 Tbsp. soy sauce
- 1 Tbsp. sesame oil

Wrappers:

- 14 oz. package round dumpling wrappers (50 wrappers; if frozen, thaw)

Serving:

- 1 cup sweet-and-sour sauce (store-bought, or from recipes on opposite page)

Directions

1. Prepare bamboo steamer baskets or pasta pot inserts by lightly oiling the surfaces the dumplings will sit on. Set baskets aside.
2. **For filling:** In a large mixing bowl, combine all ingredients for filling. Mix well to thoroughly blend.
3. **To assemble:** On a clean work surface, lay out several dumpling wrappers. Top each with 1 tablespoon of the filling mixture.
4. Moisten the edge of each wrapper with water. Fold the wrappers in half, over the filling, forming a domed half-moon.
5. Press edges together to seal. Pleat edges, if desired. Set aside.
6. Repeat process with remaining wrappers and filling.
7. Transfer finished dumplings to a steamer basket. Lay dumplings flat in a single layer, touching but not overlapping. Fill and stack additional steamer baskets as needed.
8. Add about 4 cups water to the bottom of a wok or pasta pot (water should not touch bottom of steamer basket). Add steamer baskets and lid.
9. Place pot over medium-high heat and bring water to a boil. Steam dumplings for 15 minutes, until dumplings are firm to the touch, and wrappers are somewhat translucent.
10. Serve dumplings hot, with sweet-and-sour sauce on the side for dipping.

MAKE AHEAD:

Steamed Dumplings can be made ahead and refrigerated for up to 4 days or frozen for up to 3 months. Lay cooked dumplings out in a single layer to cool completely (this will prevent them from sticking together), then package. Re-heat them in a large frying pan (thaw first if frozen). Heat the pan over medium heat, add a tablespoon or two of vegetable oil, and fry the dumplings (covered) until they are hot, browned on the bottom, and have been transformed from dumplings to potstickers (they will release from the pan when done).

VEGAN

VEGETABLE TEMPURA
Makes 12 cups

Tempura is one of my all-time favorite dishes, and my favorite way to serve it is as a meal, 1970's fondue-style, with an electric wok about half-full of hot oil in the middle of the table. I double this recipe for batter and add two pounds of protein to the mix (shrimp, haddock, tofu). The batter and dippers fill the table and we all take turns dipping and dropping bits into the oil. Paper towel-lined platters are ready to receive the fried morsels, and the evening passes as a long, luxurious, finger-food feast, as the platters pass round the table all night.

--- Ingredients ---

Vegetables:

- 8 oz. fresh mushrooms (3 cups any variety)
- 1 head broccoli
- one 8" zucchini
- 1 large white or yellow onion

(other vegetables may be substituted; 10 cups total needed)

Batter:

- 1 ¼ cup all-purpose flour
- ¼ cup cornstarch
- 1 tsp. salt
- ¼ tsp. baking soda
- 2 egg whites (if doubling recipe, use one whole egg + two egg whites)
- 1 ¼ cup cold club soda (ice water may be substituted, but the batter won't be as light)

Frying:

- 8 cups vegetable oil for deep frying (64 oz.)

Serving:

- ½ cup hot mustard sauce (store-bought or homemade from recipe on page 30)
- 1 cup sweet-and-sour sauce (store-bought or homemade Sauce #1 or #2 from recipes on page 30)

> **MAKE AHEAD:**
> Tempura can be made up to 4 days ahead of serving. Refrigerate cooked tempura, then re-heat in the oven. Spread tempura pieces out in a single layer on a baking sheet and place in a 300° oven for 10 minutes.

Directions

1. **For vegetables:** Leave small mushrooms whole and cut others in half or quarters as needed. Cut head of broccoli into individual stems. Cut zucchini into ½" thick slices. Cut onion crosswise into four thick slices and separate rings.

2. **For frying:** In a stockpot, deep frying pan, electric fryer, or wok, heat oil to 375° (a deep-fry thermometer is invaluable). Oil should be at least 3" deep. Line a baking sheet with several layers of paper towels or newspaper, lay a cooling rack upside down on top of paper, and set aside. While oil is heating, mix up batter.

3. **For batter:** In a small mixing bowl, combine flour, cornstarch, salt, and baking soda. Mix well with a fork.

4. Add the egg whites and club soda. Mix just until blended (batter will be a little lumpy).

5. Put ice cubes in the bottom of a large bowl and set the bowl of batter on top of the ice so the batter stays cold while you cook.

6. Grab one piece of broccoli with your fingers and dip it in the batter. Coat it completely and shake it to get the excess batter off. Place in the hot oil. Working quickly, add more pieces of battered broccoli to the oil, being careful to not overcrowd the pan. Cook broccoli for 6 minutes total, flipping as needed for even browning.

7. Fry one variety of vegetable at a time, so the cooking time is easy to manage. Work from the largest pieces to the smallest: broccoli first, then mushrooms, zucchini, onions, in that order. Cook each batch of food until done (broccoli and mushrooms 6 min.; zucchini 5 min.; onion rings 3 min.). Flip everything as needed for even browning.

8. Remove vegetables from oil using tongs or a kitchen spider and transfer to the prepared tray to drain.

9. Allow oil to come back up to temperature before adding the next batch of battered vegetables.

10. Transfer tempura to a serving platter and serve hot, with sauces on the side for dipping.

FRIED RICE BALLS
Makes 40 one-and-a-half inch balls

I did consider giving this recipe the awkward, but more accurate name: Fried Fried Rice Balls. Clever and tasty, these are the perfectly polite way to eat fried rice with your hands.

Ingredients

Rice:
- 1 cup brown rice
- 2 cups water

Eggs:
- 2 large eggs
- ½ tsp. soy sauce
- ½ tsp. sesame oil
- 1 tsp. butter or vegetable oil

Rice Balls:
- 2 cups thinly sliced green onions (1 grocery store bunch)
- 1 cup shelled edamame (8 oz; if frozen, thaw)
- 2 Tbsp. grated fresh ginger (peel, then grate on a microplane or the finest side of a box grater) or 1 Tbsp. ground ginger
- 1 clove garlic, finely minced and smashed into a paste (1 tsp.)
- 4 Tbsp. soy sauce
- 1 Tbsp. sesame oil
- 2 large eggs
- 1 cup plain bread or cracker crumbs

Frying:
- 8 cups vegetable oil for deep frying (64 oz.)

Directions

1. **For rice:** Place raw rice in a colander, set inside a mixing bowl. Add cold water to bowl until it covers rice. Agitate rice. Lift colander of rice out of the water to drain. Discard water.

2. Place colander of rice back in bowl and repeat rinsing process twice more. Do not skip this part, as a sticky rice is necessary for the rice balls to hold together.

3. Transfer rinsed rice to a 2-quart saucepan. Add the 2 cups water. Cover pan and place over high heat.

4. Bring rice to a boil. Stir, cover, and reduce heat to lowest possible setting.

5. Let rice cook, undisturbed, for 30 minutes. Continue with recipe while rice cooks.

6. **For eggs:** In a small bowl or mug, combine 2 eggs, soy sauce, and sesame oil and stir with a fork or whisk.

7. Place a medium frying pan over medium heat. When pan is hot, add butter or vegetable oil and swirl pan to coat the bottom and up the sides a bit.

8. Add egg mixture to pan and swirl pan so that eggs cover entire bottom of pan.

9. When eggs puff up (takes 1 - 2 minutes), flip them over, and cook on second side for 30 - 60 seconds. Remove eggs from pan and cut into pieces ½" wide and 1 - 2" long.

10. **To assemble:** When rice is done cooking, stir it vigorously to develop stickiness. Transfer rice to a large mixing bowl. Add cooked egg pieces, onions, edamame, ginger, garlic, soy sauce, and sesame oil to bowl. Stir vigorously again until everything is well blended.

11. When rice mixture has cooled to lukewarm, add raw eggs and breadcrumbs. Stir until eggs are mixed throughout and mixture binds together.

12. **For frying:** In a stockpot, deep frying pan, electric fryer, or wok, heat oil to 350° (a deep-fry thermometer is invaluable). Oil should be at least 3" deep. Line a baking sheet with several layers of paper towels or newspaper, lay a cooling rack upside down on top of paper, and set aside.

13. While oil is heating, shape rice mixture into 1 ½" balls (1 oz.), compressing the mixture as you go, so the balls won't fall apart. Lay balls on a plate or tray.

14. When oil is up to temperature, drop balls into oil. Do not crowd the pot—cook the balls in batches as needed. Cook each batch for 5 – 7 minutes total, flipping them over as needed for even browning.

15. Remove balls from oil with tongs or a kitchen spider, and place balls on prepared tray. Allow oil to come back to temperature before adding next batch.

16. Transfer fried rice balls to a bowl or platter and serve hot.

MAKE AHEAD:
Fried Rice Balls can be made ahead and refrigerated for up to 4 days or frozen for up to 3 months before serving. Thaw and lay out on a baking sheet. Re-heat in a 300° oven for 10 minutes.

GOING IT ALONE PARTY PREP COUNTDOWN

WEEKS BEFORE:
- ❏ Make Berbere Seasoning
- ❏ Make Lentil Sambusa and freeze
- ❏ Make Injera Dumplings and freeze
- ❏ Make "Meat"balls and Coconut Sauce and freeze
- ❏ Make Vegan Peanut Butter Cookies and freeze
- ❏ Make Buticha and freeze
- ❏ Make Cheeze Dip and freeze

1 WEEK BEFORE:
- ❏ Make Kolo

3 DAYS BEFORE:
- ❏ Make sauce for Awaze Tofu
- ❏ Make dip for Pineapple Sticks

2 DAYS BEFORE:
- ❏ Bake tofu for Awaze Tofu

1 DAY BEFORE:
- ❏ Make Himbasha Bread
- ❏ Get out of freezer to thaw: Lentil Sambusa, Injera Dumplings, "Meat"balls and Coconut Sauce, PB Cookies, Buticha, and Cheeze Dip

DAY OF PARTY:
Morning
- ❏ Set up food table and choose platters, bowls, and trays for serving all dishes
- ❏ Cut up pineapple (stash in fridge)
- ❏ Prep fresh vegetables and refrigerate
- ❏ Slice and toast Himbasha bread

2 Hours Before Party
- ❏ Make "Doro" Wat Bites

45 Minutes Before Party
- ❏ Re-heat in oven: Lentil Sambusa, Injera Dumplings
- ❏ Re-heat in microwave or on stovetop: "Meat"balls in Coconut Sauce, Awaze Tofu

ETHIOPIA

PARTY FOR 24

Technically .... most Ethiopian food is finger food, as so many dishes from that country are scooped up in torn pieces of injera bread, and eaten without utensils. I could have replicated here what Ethiopian restaurants serve. But I didn't. Instead, I set myself the challenge of re-interpreting Ethiopian dishes for American audiences. Ethiopians will find familiar, authentic flavors, just made in new forms. And while I was at it, I made everything vegan, with an abundance of plant-based proteins: lentils in the Sambusa, seitan in the Injera Dumplings, chickpeas in the Buticha, cashews in the Cheeze Dip, and tofu in the Awaze Tofu.

Ethiopia is an equatorial nation, so their cuisine is spicy, to thin the blood for a hot climate. What makes Ethiopian food so distinctive, though, is their use of a master spice blend called 'berbere' (BARE-bah-RAY). Complex and earthy, it is present in much of Ethiopia's cuisine, and almost every dish in this chapter, from the "Doro" Wat Bites to the Kolo Snack Mix. A recipe for berbere is included here, and gets you more than halfway to authentic.

PINEAPPLE STICKS WITH DIP

Makes 2 ½ cups dip

After perfecting this dip, I tried it with every kind of fruit that grows in Ethiopia and is available in the United States (of which there are quite a few….). I expected it to taste great with everything, but no. It is positively divine on pineapple, but meh on everything else.

Ingredients

Pineapple:

- 1 whole ripe pineapple (when ripe, a top leaf will come out easily when tugged)

Dip:

- two 8 oz. cartons Tofutti Better Than Cream Cheese (2 cups)
- ½ cup honey
- 2 Tbsp. lemon juice
- 1 tsp. cardamom
- ½ tsp. salt

Directions

1. **For pineapple:** Cut top and bottom off pineapple (about ½" thick pieces). Peel pineapple being careful to remove all of the "eyes."
2. Cut pineapple top-to-bottom in quarters. Remove tough inner core (discard).
3. Cut each quarter into 4 long wedges. Cut each wedge in thirds, making sticks that are about 3" long.
4. **For dip:** In a small mixing bowl, combine all ingredients. Stir vigorously to combine.
5. Transfer dip to a small serving bowl, set on a plate or platter. Surround dip with pineapple sticks and serve.

MAKE AHEAD:

This dip can be made up to 4 days ahead of serving. Keep covered and refrigerated.

BUTICHA (HUMMUS) WITH FRESH VEGGIES

Makes 3 cups dip

Buticha is essentially Ethiopian hummus. The spice profile of Buticha is quite different from that of Greek hummus, so traditional hummus-lovers will be surprised—I hope in a good way!

Ingredients

Dip:

- 14 oz. can chickpeas, drained and liquid reserved
- ½ cup roughly chopped red onion
- 1 large clove garlic (1 tsp.)
- 2 Tbsp. olive oil
- 2 Tbsp. peanut butter
- 1 Tbsp. lemon juice
- 4 tsp. berbere seasoning (store-bought or from recipe on page 47)
- ½ tsp. salt

Veggies:

- 2 lbs. baby carrots or carrot sticks
- 2 bell peppers, seeded and thinly sliced top to bottom
- 1 pint cherry tomatoes

Directions

1. In the container of a food processor or blender, dump all ingredients for the dip plus ½ of the reserved liquid from the chickpeas.
2. Process until smooth.
3. Add more chickpea liquid if mixture is too thick and dry, and pulse to incorporate.
4. Taste and adjust seasonings.
5. Transfer buticha to a serving bowl set on a platter surrounded by fresh vegetables for dipping.
6. **NOTE:** the remaining chickpea liquid can be stored in the refrigerator or freezer and used as a substitute for eggs (¼ cup = 1 egg) in vegan or low-cholesterol baking.

MAKE AHEAD:

Buticha can be made ahead and refrigerated for up to a week or frozen for up to 3 months. Thaw and stir before serving.

CHEEZE DIP

Makes 3 cups dip

I couldn't very well call this "cheese" dip, now could I, as it has no dairy products in it. But it does have a cheesy quality to it, so "cheeze" it is. The combination of this dip and homemade Himbasha bread is absolutely out of this world—please make both!

Ingredients

Dip:

- 14 oz. firm tofu, drained but not pressed
- 1 cup roasted, salted cashews
- 1 large clove garlic (1 tsp.)
- 3 Tbsp. nutritional yeast
- 3 Tbsp. lemon juice
- 2 Tbsp. olive oil
- 2 Tbsp. miso paste (white or red)
- 2 tsp. ground cardamom
- ½ tsp. dried oregano
- ¼ tsp. dried thyme
- ¼ tsp. salt
- ¼ tsp. ground black pepper
- ⅛ tsp. ground cayenne pepper (adds flavor, not heat)

Serving:

- 12–16 oz. package vegan flatbread or homemade Himbasha from recipe on page 44

Directions

1. **For dip:** In the container of a food processor or blender, dump all ingredients for dip.
2. Process mixture on low for 1 minute. Scrape down sides of bowl. Continue to process on high for 4–5 minutes. When done, mixture will be smooth and somewhat shiny.
3. Transfer dip to a serving bowl set on a platter surrounded by pieces of flatbread or slices of Himbasha bread or toast for scooping.

MAKE AHEAD:

Cheeze Dip can be made ahead and refrigerated for up to a week or frozen for up to 3 months. Thaw and stir before serving.

"DORO" WAT BITES
Makes 45 bite-size appetizers

In Ethiopia, doro wat is a long-simmered, spicy stew made with chunks of bone-in chicken, and finished with hard-boiled eggs. It is considered a national dish of Ethiopia and takes all day to make. Here, I have taken the principles and profiles of that dish to create a vegan version that is spicy, complex, rich, satisfying, and takes less than an hour to make.

Ingredients

Filling:

- 3 Tbsp. olive oil
- 4 cups thinly sliced white or yellow onions (3 large onions)
- 1 Tbsp. finely minced or pressed garlic (3 large cloves)
- 1 Tbsp. grated fresh ginger root (peel and grate on a microplane or the super-fine side of a box grater) or 2 tsp. ground ginger
- 1–2 Tbsp. berbere seasoning (store-bought or from recipe on page 47)
- 1 tsp. ground cardamom
- ¼ tsp. salt
- 1 cup vegetable broth or water
- 2 Tbsp. tomato paste (2 oz.)
- 10 oz. package meatless diced chik'n (vegan variety)
- 1 Tbsp. lemon juice

Shells:

- three 1.9 oz. packages phyllo pastry shells (15 shells per package)

Directions

1. **For filling:** Heat a large, deep frying pan over medium heat. Add the olive oil and swirl the pan to coat the bottom.
2. Add the onions. Cook and stir for 5 minutes, then reduce heat to low (2 on a scale of 1 to 10).
3. Cover pan. Cook onions for 30 minutes, stirring occasionally.
4. Add garlic, ginger, and berbere to onions. Stir to fully incorporate.
5. Add broth, tomato paste, and chik'n. Increase heat slightly (5 on a scale of 1 to 10) and cover.
6. Allow mixture to simmer for 10 minutes, stirring often.
7. Remove pan from heat and stir in lemon juice. Taste, and add salt if needed.
8. **To assemble:** Remove phyllo cups from packaging and arrange them on a serving platter.
9. Fill the phyllo cups with the chik'n mixture, using about ½ tablespoon filling for each. Use up all the filling and distribute equally. Serve bites immediately.

VEGAN PEANUT BUTTER COOKIES
Makes 60 two-inch cookies

Ethiopian desserts are not a thing, so Ethiopian restaurants serve "immigrant" desserts like tiramisu and cheesecake. I consider that intel to be carte blanche for me to add whatever sweet I want to this chapter. And what I want is these cookies. I concocted and made them for the first time when my brother-in-law—a long-time vegan—was visiting. I served several kinds of cookies for dessert and nearly had to taser the carnivores to keep them from eating all of these cookies before my brother-in-law got any, the cookies were just that good.

Ingredients

- 1 ½ cups natural peanut butter, preferably chunky (16 oz. jar)
- 1 cup apple sauce (2 snack cups)
- 2 ½ cups raw sugar or brown sugar
- 2 Tbsp. vanilla extract
- 2 ½ cups all-purpose flour
- 1 cup whole wheat flour
- 2 tsp. baking soda
- 1 ½ tsp. salt

MAKE AHEAD:
Vegan PB Cookies can be made ahead and stored in an airtight container at room temperature for up to 3 days or frozen for up to 12 months.

Directions

1. Preheat oven to 375°.
2. In a large mixing bowl, cream together peanut butter, applesauce, sugar, and vanilla.
3. Add remaining ingredients and mix well.
4. Shape the dough into 1" diameter balls (about 1 tablespoon each) and place on an ungreased baking sheet. Flatten the balls slightly with the tines of a fork, creating a crosshatch plus sign on the top of each cookie.
5. Bake cookies for 8 minutes.
6. Transfer cookies to a cooling rack to cool. Stack cooled cookies on a serving plate or platter and serve.

VEGAN

HIMBASHA BREAD

Makes 1 loaf

In Ethiopia, himbasha is a special-occasion bread that is served as a good luck charm for health, prosperity, safety, and a host of other blessings. It is traditionally shaped as a single, flat, round loaf, and baked in a 12" cast iron skillet. Before baking, the top is scored like a wheel with eight spokes out from the center and three concentric circles. Here, I have you shape the dough in a loaf pan to make slicing and toasting easier.

Ingredients

- 1 cup water warmed to 105°–115° (should feel like warm bath water)
- ¼ cup honey
- 1 packet active dry yeast (2 ¼ tsp.)
- ¼ cup olive oil
- 1 Tbsp. nigella seeds or black sesame seeds
- 2 tsp. ground cardamom
- 1 ½ tsp. salt
- 1 tsp. ground coriander
- 3 cups bread flour

Directions

1. In a large mixing bowl, combine water, honey, and yeast. Stir gently, then let mixture sit for 5 minutes for yeast to dissolve and activate.
2. Add remaining ingredients. Mix with a sturdy spoon and then with your hands until all the flour is incorporated and a dough forms.
3. Transfer the dough to a work surface and knead it for 5 minutes, until the dough is smooth and elastic. Dough should be soft but not sticky. Add more flour if needed.
4. Grease the mixing bowl with oil or spray oil, and return dough to bowl. Turn and flip the dough so all sides are covered with oil.
5. Cover bowl with a damp towel and set to rise until doubled in bulk (60–90 minutes).
6. When dough has risen and doubled in size, punch dough down. Knead dough to get the air out. Shape dough into a loaf. Place loaf in a greased bread pan.
7. Cover pan with the damp towel, and set in a warm place to rise a second time for 60 minutes.
8. Preheat oven to 350°.
9. Bake bread for 25–35 minutes. When done, loaf will sound hollow when tapped on the bottom. Remove bread from pan to cool.
10. If serving the bread fresh from the oven to accompany Cheeze Dip (recipe on preceding page), cut bread into 1" x 1" x 2" pieces. Otherwise, slice and toast the bread, then X-cut each slice into four triangular toast points before serving with dip.

MAKE AHEAD:

Himbasha Bread can be made up to 4 days ahead of serving. And Himbasha toast points can be made 1 day before serving. Keep in a ziptop bag or tightly covered container at room temperature.

VEGAN

AWAZE TOFU
Makes 5 cups

Awaze seasoning is a paste made from wine, oil, and berbere seasoning. Here, I have sauced that up a bit, making a spicy, sweet-and-sour-y coating for tofu.

Ingredients

Tofu:

- three 14 oz. packages extra firm tofu, drained
- 3 Tbsp. soy sauce
- 3 Tbsp. vegetable oil
- 3 Tbsp. cornstarch

Sauce:

- 2 Tbsp. olive oil
- ½ cup finely minced white or yellow onion (½ of a small onion)
- 5 large cloves garlic, finely minced or pressed (5 tsp.)
- 1 Tbsp. grated fresh ginger root (peel and grate on a microplane or the super-fine side of a box grater) or 2 tsp. ground ginger
- 1 Tbsp. berbere seasoning (store-bought or from recipe on page 47)
- 8 oz. can tomato sauce (1 cup; plain, not pasta sauce)
- ¼ cup dry, red wine (Cabernet Sauvignon or Merlot)
- 2 Tbsp. honey
- 1 Tbsp. lemon juice
- 1 tsp. salt

Directions

1. **For tofu:** Cut each block of tofu horizontally into three 4" x 6" slabs. Lay slabs out flat on several layers of paper towel or a folded tea towel, and top with more paper towels or another tea towel.
2. Place a baking sheet or cutting board on top of the tofu, and weigh it down (cans of food work great). Let sit at least 30 minutes, to press excess moisture out of the tofu.
3. Preheat oven to 400°.
4. Cut tofu slabs into 9 pieces each (3 rows x 3 columns). Transfer pieces to a large mixing bowl. Add soy sauce and oil. Using a rubber spatula, gently stir to coat tofu.
5. Add cornstarch. Gently stir until tofu is coated and no white spots of cornstarch remain. (Don't add the soy sauce, oil, and cornstarch all at once—it will make a gloppy mess.)
6. Transfer tofu to a greased baking sheet, laying the cubes out flat, in a single layer.
7. Bake tofu for 30–45 minutes, flipping pieces over in the middle of baking time (tofu should be lightly browned on both sides). While tofu is baking, prepare sauce.
8. **For sauce:** Place a 3-quart saucepan over medium heat. Add the olive oil and swirl pan to coat the bottom.
9. Add the onions, garlic, and ginger to the pan. Sauté until the onions are translucent (about 5 minutes).
10. Add berbere and stir in. Sauté until fragrant (less than a minute).
11. Add the tomato sauce, wine, honey, lemon juice, and salt to the pan. Stir. Cover, reduce heat to low, and simmer sauce for 5 minutes. Turn heat off and leave pan on warm burner until tofu is baked.
12. Add the cooked tofu to the sauce and stir gently to coat pieces. Transfer tofu to a serving bowl and serve with fork picks or toothpicks.

MAKE AHEAD:
This dish can be prepared up to 4 days ahead of serving. Keep the tofu and sauce separate in covered containers in the refrigerator. Combine and re-heat just before serving.

"MEAT" BALLS IN COCONUT SAUCE
Makes 30 one-inch balls

The sauce on these meatballs is full-flavored, but not hot and spicy like most everything else in this chapter. This dish provides a wonderful counterpoint to the rest of the menu, and something for the heat-averse to love.

Ingredients

Meatballs:

- 16 oz. package meatless ground beef (vegan; as for burgers)
- 8 oz. package tempeh, crumbled
- 1 Tbsp. onion powder
- 1 Tbsp. finely minced or pressed garlic (3 large cloves) or 1 ½ tsp. garlic powder
- 1 Tbsp. soy sauce
- 1 tsp. liquid smoke
- ½ tsp. coriander
- ¼ tsp. salt

Sauce:

- 2 Tbsp. vegetable oil
- 1 red onion, finely minced (2 cups)
- 1 Tbsp. grated fresh ginger root (peel and grate on a microplane or the super-fine side of a box grater) or 2 tsp. ground ginger
- 1 Tbsp. finely minced or pressed garlic (3 large cloves)
- 2 tsp. berbere seasoning (store-bought or from recipe on opposite page)
- 1 tsp. ground turmeric
- 1 large beefsteak tomato, diced (1 ½ cups)
- 1 cup coconut milk
- 1 Tbsp. tomato paste
- ½ tsp. salt

VEGAN

Directions

1. **For meatballs:** Preheat oven to 400°.
2. In a large mixing bowl, combine all meatball ingredients. Mix with hands to fully incorporate seasonings.
3. Form mixture into 1" balls (a ⅔ oz. cookie scoop works great for this) and place on a greased baking sheet.
4. Bake meatballs for 20 minutes. While meatballs bake, prepare sauce.
5. **For sauce:** Place a 3-quart saucepan over medium heat. When pan is hot, add oil, onion, ginger, and garlic. Sauté until onions are soft and just beginning to brown (about 10 minutes). Stir occasionally.
6. Add berbere and turmeric. Stir in.
7. Add remaining ingredients for sauce. Stir and cover. Reduce heat to low (2 on a scale of 1 to 10) and simmer sauce for 20 minutes. Stir occasionally.
8. Add cooked balls to sauce. Gently stir to coat. Allow mixture to stay over heat until heated through, then transfer to a serving bowl. Serve meatballs with forked picks or toothpicks.

MAKE AHEAD:
"Meat"balls in Coconut Sauce can be made ahead and refrigerated for up to 4 days or frozen for up to 3 months. Keep the balls and sauce in separate containers. Combine and re-heat just before serving.

BERBERE SEASONING
Makes ¾ cup

Berbere seasoning is Ethiopian in origin and found in a great many dishes from that country. Sometimes sold in paste form, here this spicy, complex seasoning comes to you as a dry mix, ready to be added to all manner of things, or used on its own as a dry rub for fish or shrimp.

Ingredients

- 2 Tbsp. chili powder
- 2 Tbsp. smoked paprika
- 1 Tbsp. ground cayenne pepper
- 1 Tbsp. garlic powder
- 1 Tbsp. onion powder
- 1 Tbsp. ground ginger
- 2 tsp. salt
- 1 tsp. fenugreek powder or 1 tsp. ground celery seed + ½ tsp. ground cumin
- 1 tsp. ground coriander
- 1 tsp. cardamom
- 1 tsp. ground thyme
- ½ tsp. ground cinnamon
- ½ tsp. ground black pepper
- ¼ tsp. ground cloves

Directions

1. In a small bowl, combine all ingredients and mix with a whisk.
2. Transfer spice blend to an airtight container and label. Store at room temperature.
3. Seasoning blend will maintain its flavor for a year at room temperature and longer if stored in the freezer.

KOLO SNACK MIX
Makes 6 cups

Kolo is a traditional Ethiopian snack made of a crunchy mix of roasted, spiced nuts, seeds, beans, and barley. There are many variations on the "traditional," so I took liberties here. Mine features dabo (a sort of spicy Ethiopian pretzel), and a variety of unorthodox substitutions for us American cooks who shop in American grocery stores. Think of it as my crazy delicious American interpretation of kolo.

--- Ingredients ---

Dabo:

- 1 ½ cups whole wheat flour
- ½ cup corn meal
- 1 Tbsp. berbere seasoning (store-bought or from recipe on page 47)
- 2 tsp. granulated sugar
- 1 tsp. salt
- ⅔ cup water
- ¼ cup olive oil

Nuts and Grains Mixture:

- 1 cup Grape Nuts original cereal
- 1 cup peanuts
- ½ cup sunflower seeds
- 5 oz. bag crunchy sea salt chickpea snacks

Finishing:

- 2 Tbsp. olive oil
- 1 Tbsp. berbere seasoning
- ½ tsp. salt

Directions

1. **For Dabo:** In a medium mixing bowl, combine all ingredients. Mix with hands and knead until a smooth dough forms. If dough is crumbly, add more water, 1 tablespoon at a time.
2. Let dough rest for 10 minutes.
3. Preheat oven to 375°.
4. Divide dough into six or eight pieces and roll each piece into a long rope. Roll ropes until they are the diameter of a thick pencil or the end of your pinky finger.
5. Cut ropes of dough into pieces that are as long as they are wide. The cut pieces should resemble little square pillows. Scatter pieces across a baking sheet (they can touch but shouldn't be piled).
6. Bake dabo for 25–30 minutes, shaking or stirring the pieces every 10 minutes. When done, pieces will be crispy. While dabo are baking, prepare nuts and grains mixture.
7. **For nuts and grains:** Place a 10" skillet over medium heat. When pan is hot, add Grape Nuts. Roast cereal, stirring constantly, for 2 minutes. Transfer cereal to a large mixing bowl.
8. Immediately add the finishing oil, berbere, and salt to the warmed cereal. Stir until the cereal is evenly coated.
9. Place the skillet back over medium heat. Add the peanuts. Roast until nuts are lightly browned and fragrant (about 3 minutes), stirring constantly. Add nuts to cereal in bowl.
10. In the same frying pan, roast the sunflower seeds until they are lightly browned and fragrant (about 2 minutes). Stir constantly. Add roasted seeds to bowl.
11. Add chickpeas and baked dabo to mixture in bowl. Toss to combine ingredients and distribute seasoning.
12. Serve kolo immediately or store in an airtight container, at room temperature.

MAKE AHEAD:
Kolo can be made up to a week before serving.

INJERA DUMPLINGS
Makes 30 one-and-a-half inch dumplings

You have to plan ahead for these, as the injera batter has to sit at room temperature and ferment for 4 to 24 hours. The good news is that you can make them well ahead of party time, refrigerate or freeze them, and re-heat them right before guests arrive. The classic injera bread flavor combined with Ethiopian-spiced plant-based protein makes these dumplings a powerhouse of regional flavors!

---— Ingredients ———

Batter:

- 1 cup teff flour or whole wheat flour (not stone ground)
- ½ cup rye flour
- ½ cup all-purpose flour
- 1 tsp. baking soda
- ½ tsp. salt
- 1 ½ cups club soda
- ¼ cup plain vegan yogurt (if you have a choice, avoid coconut-based)
- 1 Tbsp. vegetable oil

Seitan:

- 8 oz. package plain seitan strips, cut in ½" dice
- 1 cup finely minced red onion (½ large onion)
- 1 Tbsp. grated fresh ginger root (peel and grate on a microplane or the super-fine side of a box grater) or 2 tsp. ground ginger
- 2 large cloves garlic (2 tsp.), minced and smashed to a paste with ½ tsp. salt
- 3 Tbsp. berbere seasoning (store-bought or from recipe on page 47)
- 1 tsp. brown mustard

Frying:

- 8 cups vegetable oil for deep frying (64 oz.)

VEGAN

Directions

1. **For batter:** In a large mixing bowl, combine flours, baking soda, and salt. Whisk to thoroughly combine.
2. Add club soda, yogurt, and oil. Mix to make a smooth, thin batter.
3. Cover bowl with a tea towel and let sit at room temperature for 4–24 hours (longer is better).
4. **For seitan:** After batter has rested and fermented, prepare seitan. In a separate, medium mixing bowl, combine all ingredients for seitan. Stir gently to coat everything in seasonings.
5. Add seitan mixture to batter and fold in.
6. **For frying:** In a stockpot, deep frying pan, electric fryer, or wok, heat oil to 350° (a deep-fry thermometer is invaluable). Oil should be at least 3" deep. Line a baking sheet with several layers of paper towels or newspaper, lay a cooling rack upside down on top of paper, and set aside.
7. When oil is up to temperature, drop batter by 1 tablespoon scoopfuls into oil (a ⅔ oz. cookie scoop works great for this). Do not crowd the pot—cook in batches as needed. Cook each batch for 5 minutes total, flipping dumplings over as needed for even browning. Remove cooked dumplings from oil using tongs or a kitchen spider. Lay on prepared tray to drain.
8. Allow oil to come back up to temperature before adding next batch of batter.
9. Transfer finished injera dumplings to a serving bowl or platter and serve hot.

MAKE AHEAD:
Injera Dumplings can be made ahead and refrigerated for up to a week or frozen for up to 3 months. Thaw and lay out on a baking sheet. Re-heat in a 300° oven for 10 minutes.

LENTIL SAMBUSA
Makes 40 appetizer-sized pies

Ethiopian Sambusa are appetizer-sized fried turnovers, similar to Indian samosa. Cute, spicy, and delicious, they will undoubtably be the hit of any party. It takes a minute to get the hang of shaping and sealing them, so allow yourself extra time the first time you make these, and don't be shy about asking for help, with one person in charge of the frying while the rest assemble. You may begin to wonder if they are worth the trouble, but I promise, they totally are.

--- Ingredients ---

Filling:

- 2 Tbsp. olive oil
- 1 cup finely diced white or yellow onion (1 medium onion)
- 1 cup finely diced green bell pepper (1 pepper)
- 1 jalapeño pepper, finely minced (seeds in for heat, seeds out for not)
- 3 large cloves garlic, finely minced or pressed (1 Tbsp.)
- 1 Tbsp. grated fresh ginger root (peel and grate on a microplane or the super-fine side of a box grater) or 2 tsp. ground ginger
- 2 tsp. ground cardamom
- 2 tsp. ground coriander
- 1 tsp. ground cinnamon
- 1 tsp. salt
- 1 tsp. ground black pepper
- 1 ¼ cups green or brown lentils, rinsed (10 oz.)
- 2 ½ cups vegetable broth or water

Dough:

- 2 ½ cups all-purpose flour
- ½ cup whole wheat flour
- 1 tsp. salt
- 1 cup warm water
- 2 Tbsp. olive oil

Frying:

- 8 cups vegetable oil for deep frying (64 oz.)

Directions

1. **For filling:** Place a 2-quart saucepan over medium-high heat. Add the olive oil and swirl the pan to coat the bottom.
2. Add the onions, peppers, garlic, ginger, and spices to the pot. Sauté until the onions are translucent (about 5 minutes).
3. Add the lentils and broth to the pot. Cover and bring to a boil.
4. Stir, reduce heat to low, and simmer until water is absorbed and lentils are tender (about 45 minutes).
5. While lentil mixture is cooking, prepare dough.
6. **For dough:** In a medium mixing bowl, combine dry ingredients for dough. Mix.
7. Add water and oil. Mix with hands until a stiff dough forms.
8. Transfer dough to a work surface and knead until dough is smooth (2-5 minutes).
9. Return dough to mixing bowl, cover with a damp towel, and let rest for 30 minutes.
10. When lentils are cooked, transfer them to a broad bowl or baking pan to facilitate cooling.
11. When dough is ready and lentils are cool enough to handle, start heating oil.
12. **For frying:** In a stockpot, deep frying pan, electric fryer, or wok, heat oil to 350° (a deep-fry thermometer is invaluable). Oil should be at least 3" deep. Line a baking sheet with several layers of paper towels or newspaper, lay a cooling rack upside down on top of paper, and set aside.
13. **To assemble:** Roll dough out into a thick snake and cut it into 20 equal portions. Using a rolling pin, flatten one portion of dough out into a 5" disk. Cut disk in half.
14. Place 1 tablespoon of lentil filling on each semicircle of dough.
15. With the centerpoint of the straight edge forming the point of a cone, fold the straight edge of one semicircle in half and pinch the straight edge together over the filling. This will create a raised seam and a cone shape with filling inside.
16. With the raised seam on the top of the sambusa, tuck the filling in and pinch the open edge closed.
17. Repeat this process with the remaining dough and filling.
18. When the oil is up to temperature, drop sambusa into oil. Do not crowd the pot—cook in batches as needed. Cook each batch for 4–5 minutes total, flipping sambusa over as needed for even browning. Remove cooked sambusa from oil using tongs or a kitchen spider. Lay on prepared tray to drain.
19. Allow oil to come back up to temperature before adding next batch of sambusa.
20. Transfer finished sambusas to a serving bowl or platter and serve hot.

MAKE AHEAD:

Sambusas can be made ahead and refrigerated for up to 4 days or frozen for up to 3 months. Thaw and lay out on a baking sheet. Re-heat in a 300° oven for 10 minutes.

VEGAN

GOING IT ALONE
PARTY PREP COUNTDOWN

WEEKS BEFORE:
- ❏ Make Gougères dough and freeze
- ❏ Make Salmon Croquettes and freeze
- ❏ Make Sablé Breton Cookies and freeze

4 DAYS BEFORE:
- ❏ Cook onions for Cheese Tart
- ❏ Make French Onion Dip

3 DAYS BEFORE:
- ❏ Make crêpes for Sausages in Crêpes
- ❏ Make Chocolate-Hazelnut Dip

2 DAYS BEFORE:
- ❏ Make Shrimp Provençal
- ❏ Make Crab Quiche Bites

1 DAY BEFORE:
- ❏ Make Beurre Blanc Deviled Eggs
- ❏ Make Socca flatbreads
- ❏ Make Stuffed Mushrooms but do not bake
- ❏ Make filling for Lobster Thermidors
- ❏ Remove from freezer to thaw: Salmon Croquettes, Sablé Breton Cookies

DAY OF PARTY:
Morning
- ❏ Get Gougères dough out of freezer and onto a baking sheet
- ❏ Set up food table and choose platters, bowls, and trays for serving all dishes
- ❏ Prep fresh vegetables and refrigerate

2 Hours Before Party
- ❏ Bake Gougères
- ❏ Make Cheese Tart
- ❏ Bake sausages for crêpes; wrap & warm crêpes in oven

1 Hour Before Party
- ❏ Assemble Sausages in Crêpes
- ❏ Bake Stuffed Mushrooms
- ❏ Assemble and bake Lobster Thermidors
- ❏ Re-heat in oven: Socca, Salmon Croquettes, Crab Quiche Bites

54 PARTY ON!

FRANCE

PARTY FOR 30

French food is naturally rather elegant, which is lovely when you are planning a more refined get-together. All those classic preparations! All that French cheese! All those succulent shellfish! This particular collection of French finger foods also happens to be the most brunchy of all the chapters in this book, with a menu that includes Beurre Blanc Deviled Eggs, Sausages in Crêpes, and Crab Quiche Bites. The complete menu lends itself to an early-in-the-day special occasion, an afternoon tea, a pre-event noshing, or any celebration that is a cut above jeans and t-shirts. In the spirit of full disclosure, it also happens to be the toughest chapter to manage completely on your own because of the demands on your oven in the final crunch. Ideally, you would have co-hosts for a full-chapter party, and a split of that last-minute list. But … . if you have good time management skills along with double ovens or a convection oven plus a large toaster oven (one that accommodates a 12" pizza), you should do just fine.

SHRIMP PROVENÇAL

Makes 6 cups

French food can be a bit heavy on the butter and cream, so these shrimp are a welcome addition to any buffet of French foods. Light and fresh, they contrast and complement other recipes in this chapter. And if you are aren't making this whole chapter, but are in search of a simple dish to share, they are wonderful on their own.

Ingredients

- 4 lbs. raw, peeled, de-veined, tail-on shrimp (any size)
- 1 Tbsp. finely minced or pressed garlic (3 large cloves)
- ¼ cup sundried tomatoes in oil (2 oz.), drained and finely diced
- 3 Tbsp. oil from sundried tomatoes jar
- 1 Tbsp. lemon juice
- 1 Tbsp. onion powder
- 2 tsp. dried thyme
- 2 tsp. dried basil
- 1 tsp. dried parsley
- ½ tsp. salt
- ¼ tsp. red pepper flakes

MAKE AHEAD:
Shrimp Provençal can be made up to 2 days ahead of serving. Keep covered and refrigerated. Serve at room temperature.

Directions

1. Preheat oven to 350°.
2. In a large mixing bowl, combine all ingredients. Stir gently until shrimp are evenly coated in oil and seasonings.
3. Transfer shrimp to a 9" x 13" baking pan. Spread shrimp out to an even layer.
4. Bake shrimp for 15–20 minutes, depending on their size. Stir once in the middle of baking time. Shrimp will be pink, opaque, and firm when done.
5. Transfer shrimp to a serving bowl and serve hot or at room temperature.

SEAFOOD

CHEESE PLATE WITH SOCCA

Makes 32 flatbread wedges

For me, socca flatbreads are a great culinary mystery. The batter for them tastes dreadful, but cooked socca are absolutely marvelous. How can that be? Crispy on the outside, soft on the inside, they are the perfect complement to cheese. Socca do not keep well, though, so don't make them more than a day ahead of serving.

Ingredients

Socca:

- 1 cup chickpea flour
- ½ tsp. dried thyme or tarragon
- ½ tsp. garlic powder
- ½ tsp. salt
- ½ tsp. ground black pepper
- 1 cup hot water
- ¼ cup olive oil + 1 Tbsp. olive oil for frying

Cheese Plate:

- 8 oz. block of each of three or four kinds of French cheese: one soft (Boursin, Brie, or Camembert), one or two hard (Comte, Emmental, Gruyere, or Mimolette), and one veined (bleu or Roquefort)

MAKE AHEAD:
Socca can be made 1 day ahead of serving. Store in an airtight bag or container. Re-crisp on a baking sheet in a 350° oven for 10 minutes. Do not cut flatbreads into wedges until after re-crisping.

Directions

1. **For socca:** In a medium mixing bowl, combine flour and seasonings. Mix well.
2. Add water and ¼ cup oil to bowl and whisk to form a smooth batter. Let batter rest for 30 minutes.
3. Preheat oven to 500°, with an 8" cast iron skillet inside.
4. **For cheese plate:** While batter rests and oven heats, prepare cheese plate. Arrange cheeses on a plate or cheese board, leaving room for piles of socca. Add knives for spreading and slicing the cheeses.
5. When oven is up to temperature and pan is blazing hot, remove pan. Add about a teaspoon of the remaining oil to the pan and swirl to coat the bottom.
6. Pour ½ cup batter into hot pan. Tilt pan to distribute batter in an even layer. Return pan to oven and bake for 6–10 minutes. Edges of flatbread should be browned and crispy.
7. Remove pan from oven and transfer socca to a cutting board. Repeat oiling and cooking process with remaining batter.
8. Slice each socca into 8 wedges. Add wedges to the cheese plate and serve. Refrigerate any leftovers.

VEGETARIAN

FRENCH ONION DIP WITH FRESH VEGETABLES

Makes 3 cups dip

Yes, you can make onion dip really fast with one of those pouches of soup mix. But what you end up with is a dip that tastes a lot like the box it came out of. This dip, by contrast, is made from real ingredients and tastes like it came out of your garden. Or heaven. Or your garden in heaven. If you are making this for a full-chapter-party, stick with the veggie tray, but if you are making this dip as a one-off to take to a random party, it is also incredible on potato chips.

Ingredients

Caramelized onions:

- 1 Tbsp. vegetable oil
- 1 tsp. butter
- 3 cups diced white or yellow onions (1 lb.)

Dip:

- 4 oz. block cream cheese, at room temperature
- ½ cup sour cream
- ¼ cup mayonnaise
- ¼ cup finely minced green onions (1–2 onions)
- ½ tsp. salt
- ½ tsp. vegetarian Worcestershire sauce

Veggies:

- 2 lbs. baby carrots or carrot sticks
- 2 cucumbers, sliced (6"–8" each)
- 1 pint cherry tomatoes

MAKE AHEAD:
French Onion Dip can be made up to 5 days ahead of serving. Keep covered and refrigerated. Serve cold or at room temperature.

Directions

1. **For onions:** Add oil and butter to a large frying pan over medium heat.
2. Add onions and sauté until onions are translucent and just barely beginning to color (about 10 minutes). Stir frequently.
3. Reduce heat to low (3 on a scale of 1 to 10), and continue cooking for 30 minutes. Stir occasionally. Onions should be caramelized, evenly browned, and reduced in volume to less than 2 cups.
4. **For dip:** In a medium mixing bowl, combine cream cheese, sour cream, and mayonnaise. Mix with a whisk until smooth.
5. Add green onion, salt, and Worcestershire. Mix in.
6. Add caramelized onions and gently fold in. Transfer dip to a serving bowl set on a platter, surrounded by fresh vegetables for dipping.

CHOCOLATE-HAZELNUT DIP WITH COOKIES & FRUIT

Makes 6 cups dip

People will lose their minds and any self-control they may have once had over this. Seriously. Six cups of the stuff may seem like a lot, but trust me, it isn't.

Ingredients

Dip:

- two 8 oz. blocks cream cheese, at room temperature
- two 13 oz. jars Nutella Hazelnut Spread (2 cups)
- 1 ½ cups powdered sugar, sifted
- ½ cup baking cocoa, sifted
- 1 ½ cups heavy cream

Serving:

- 11 oz. box Nilla Wafers or homemade Sablé Breton Cookies from recipe on facing page
- 2 lbs. fresh strawberries, rinsed and patted dry (6 cups)

Directions

1. **For dip:** In a large mixing bowl, combine the cream cheese and Nutella. With a wooden spoon or hand mixer, mix until the two become one.
2. Add remaining ingredients. Mix until smooth.
3. Transfer dip to a serving bowl set on a platter. Serve immediately, surrounded by cookies and strawberries, or cover dip and refrigerate until needed.

MAKE AHEAD:
Chocolate-Hazelnut Dip can be made up to a week ahead of serving. Keep dip tightly covered and refrigerated. Allow dip to come to room temperature before serving (dip will soften to a dipping consistency as it warms).

SABLÉ BRETON COOKIES

Makes 75 bite-sized cookies

These classic, French butter cookies are so simple and yet so sublime—great on their own or as scoops for the Chocolate-Hazelnut Dip featured on the facing page.

Ingredients

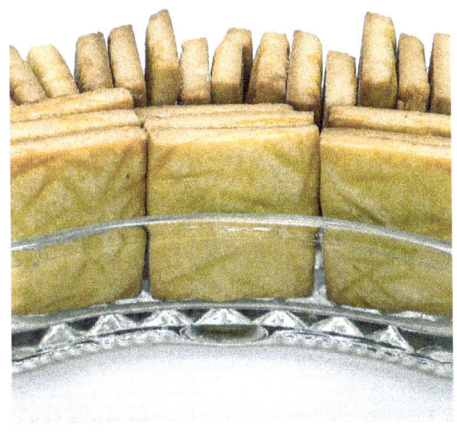

Dough:

- 1 cup butter, at room temperature (2 sticks)
- ⅔ cup granulated sugar
- 1 large egg + 1 egg yolk
- 2 tsp. vanilla extract
- 2 ⅔ cups all-purpose flour
- 3 Tbsp. cornstarch
- ½ tsp. salt

Egg Wash:

- 1 egg yolk
- 1 Tbsp. milk

Directions

1. Preheat oven to 350°.
2. In a large mixing bowl, beat the butter and sugar together until smooth and fluffy. Add the egg, egg yolk, and vanilla. Mix in (mixture should look curdled).
3. Add the dry ingredients. Mix with a spoon and then with hands to incorporate flour fully.
4. Gather the dough and shape it into a flat square. Place it on a well-floured work surface. Lightly sprinkle flour over top. With a rolling pin, roll the dough out to ¼" thickness (thick end of a chopstick). Keep the dough as square or rectangular as possible.
5. Using a patterned rolling pin, the side of a whisk, or another interesting food-safe item, gently press a pattern into the dough.
6. In a mug or ramekin, beat the egg yolk and milk for the egg wash. Brush the yolk mixture over top of the patterned dough.
7. Using a sharp knife or rolling pizza cutter, cut the dough into 1 ½" squares. If making these for a fancy occasion, trim off the irregular edges of dough first (bake and eat those bits yourself), so all the cookies have straight sides. Transfer squares of dough to ungreased baking sheets, leaving a small space between them.
8. Bake cookies 11–12 minutes, until they are beginning to brown. Transfer cookies to a cooling rack and allow them to cool completely.
9. Serve cookies on their own, or to accompany the chocolate dip on the facing page.

MAKE AHEAD:
Sablé Breton Cookies can be made a week ahead of serving if kept tightly covered at room temperature, or up to 3 months ahead if frozen.

STUFFED MUSHROOMS

Makes 30 - 40

Turns out, there's a reason that the classic way of making stuffed mushrooms is still the gold standard. I tried stuffing all manner of things into and onto mushroom caps, to delicious but disastrous result. Nothing cooked at the right rate, fillings dried out and/ or fell out, and eating any of my trials as finger food was laughable. So, a French tweak of the classic it is … .

Ingredients

Mushrooms:

- 2 lbs. baby bella, small, whole portobello mushrooms

Stuffing:

- 1 cup Italian-style bread crumbs
- ¼ cup olive oil
- 5 oz. package smoky tempeh or other vegetarian bacon, finely diced
- 3 large cloves garlic, finely minced or pressed (1 Tbsp.)
- 3 large eggs
- 1 tsp. dried marjoram
- ½ tsp. salt

MAKE AHEAD:
Mushrooms can be assembled through step #5 the day before baking and serving. Keep covered and refrigerated.

Directions

1. Preheat oven to 350°.
2. Wash mushrooms and remove stems. Finely dice half of the mushroom stems (reserve remaining stems for another purpose).
3. **For stuffing:** In a small mixing bowl, combine bread crumbs and oil. Stir until crumbs are evenly moist.
4. Add diced mushroom stems plus remaining ingredients for stuffing to bowl. Stir well to combine.
5. Fill each mushroom cap with the breadcrumb mixture. This is best achieved with your hands—hold a mushroom cap over the bowl of stuffing and press the mixture in and on the mushroom. The stuffing should be generously mounded up on each mushroom, and used up.
6. Place stuffed mushroom caps on a greased baking sheet.
7. Bake mushrooms for 25–30 minutes. Don't over-do it — over-cooking makes them hard to pick up and eat.
8. Transfer mushrooms to a serving platter and serve hot.

SALMON CROQUETTES

Makes 30 one-inch balls

It took about a thousand trials to get these right, and I am glad that I persisted. Early test batches were not at all what I was going for. But the cookbook-worthy croquettes from the recipe below are all that I dreamed of: crispy on the outside, moist and tender on the inside, and positively scrumptious.

Ingredients

Croquettes:

- two 7.1 oz. pouches or three 5 oz. pouches or three 5 oz. cans pink salmon, drained (boneless, skinless)
- 1 cup very finely minced celery (2–3 stalks) or grated celeriac root
- 1 cup very finely minced red onion or thinly sliced green onions (4–6 onions)
- ¼ cup corn meal
- ¼ cup heavy cream
- 2 large eggs
- 1 Tbsp. Worcestershire sauce
- 1–4 tsp. prepared horseradish (brands vary)
- ½ tsp. salt

Breading:

- 1 cup bread or cracker crumbs
- ¼ cup olive oil

Serving:

- 1 cup Sriracha mayonnaise (store-bought or homemade: 1 cup mayonnaise + 1 Tbsp. Sriracha hot chili sauce)

MAKE AHEAD:
Salmon Croquettes can be made ahead of serving—up to 3 days ahead if refrigerated, and up to 3 months if frozen. Thaw and re-heat on a baking sheet in a 350° oven for 10 minutes.

Directions

1. Preheat oven to 400°.
2. In a medium mixing bowl, combine ingredients for croquettes, using the smallest amount of horseradish.
3. Stir mixture with a fork, until salmon is flaked into small pieces and mixture is well blended. Smell mixture. If no hint of horseradish is present, add another teaspoon and mix in. Repeat this until the hint is there.
4. In a small bowl, combine ingredients for breading. Mix until crumbs are evenly moist.
5. Shape salmon mixture into heaping-tablespoon balls (a ⅔ oz. cookie scoop works great for this).
6. Drop balls into breading mixture and roll to coat in crumbs. Place balls on a greased baking sheet, leaving ½" space between them.
7. Bake salmon croquettes for 15–20 minutes, until lightly browned.
8. Transfer croquettes to a serving bowl or platter. Serve with Sriracha mayo on the side for dipping.

SEAFOOD

CRAB QUICHE BITES

Makes 60 tartlets

I am uncommonly happy in my marriage, but if I ever find myself in need of a second husband, I want these served at my wedding reception.

Ingredients

Filling:

- 8 oz. cream cheese, at room temperature
- 3 large eggs
- 8 oz. lump crab meat or three 6 oz. cans lump crab, drained
- 14 oz. can artichoke hearts, drained and finely chopped
- ½ cup thinly sliced green onions (2–4 onions) or finely minced red onion
- 2 Tbsp. capers, roughly chopped
- ½ tsp. prepared horseradish
- ½ tsp. seasoned salt

Shells:

- four 1.9 oz. packages frozen mini phyllo pastry shells (15 shells per package; no need to thaw)

> **MAKE AHEAD:**
> Crab Quiche Bites can be made up to 2 days ahead of serving. Keep covered and refrigerated. Re-heat on a baking sheet in a 350° oven for 10 minutes.

Directions

1. Preheat oven to 350°.
2. In a medium mixing bowl, place cream cheese. Soften it by stirring and smushing it with a sturdy spatula or the back of a wooden spoon.
3. Add eggs, one at a time, and incorporate them into the cream cheese with a whisk or hand mixer. Stir until the mixture is smooth.
4. Add remaining ingredients for filling and stir with the spatula or spoon until blended.
5. Remove pastry shells from packaging and transfer them to a baking sheet (shells may touch).
6. Fill the pastry shells with the filling, distributing filling evenly and using it all up. Shells should be over-full, with the filling mounded.
7. Bake bites for 25 minutes.
8. Transfer crab bites to a serving platter and serve warm.

SEAFOOD

SAUSAGES IN CRÊPES

Makes 24 - 30 cigar-shaped appetizers

This crêpe batter is lovely, very agreeable, and easy for a novice cook to work with. With bravado, you can actually have two pans going at once when cooking these up. If you are a first-timer, make a few practice crêpes first, then go for it.

Ingredients

Crêpe Batter:

- 1 cup whole milk (or ¾ cup skim milk + ¼ cup heavy cream)
- 3 large eggs
- ⅔ cup buckwheat flour
- ⅓ cup all-purpose flour
- 1 tsp. granulated sugar
- ½ tsp. salt
- 4 Tbsp. melted butter, cooled slightly
- ½ cup thinly sliced green onions (2–4 onions)

Frying:

- 2 Tbsp. butter

Filling:

- 24 oz. veggie breakfast sausage links (24–30 links)
- ¼ cup dijon mustard

MAKE AHEAD:
Crêpes can be made through step #10 up to 3 days ahead of serving. Store in an airtight bag or container in the refrigerator. Wrap stack of crêpes in aluminum foil and warm in oven while sausages bake.

Directions

1. **For crêpes:** In a medium mixing bowl, combine milk and eggs. Stir vigorously with a whisk to combine.
2. Add flours, sugar, and salt. Stir until smooth.
3. Drizzle in the butter while stirring. Add onions and mix in.
4. Set batter aside and allow to rest for 30 minutes.
5. Preheat oven to 375°.
6. Heat an 8" skillet over medium heat.
7. When skillet is hot, swirl ½ teaspoon butter around to coat pan.
8. Add 1 ½ tablespoons batter to pan and immediately swirl pan so batter forms a 5" disc. Use a calibrated ladle or cookie scoop (1 ounce) so all the crêpes turn out the same size. Cook crêpe about 1 minute on the first side. Edges of crêpe should look dry and begin to curl.
9. With a heat-proof rubber or silicone spatula, flip crêpe over. Cook about 30 seconds on second side. Remove crêpe to a plate.
10. Repeat buttering and cooking process until batter is used up. Stack cooked crêpes on plate.
11. **For filling:** While crêpes cook, bake sausages according to package instructions.
12. **To assemble:** Spread ½ teaspoon mustard on the less attractive side of a crêpe. Place a sausage on top and roll the crêpe around it. Repeat process with remaining ingredients. Stack rolled crêpes on a plate or platter and serve.

VEGETARIAN

BEURRE BLANC DEVILED EGGS

Makes 30 egg halves

It is rare to have an idea for a dish that is truly original, but these come dangerously close. Rich, distinctive, and unique, taste-testers said they'd never had deviled eggs like this before, then came back for seconds and thirds until the platter was cleared.

Ingredients

Eggs:

- 15 large eggs, hard-boiled and cooled

Beurre Blanc:

- ½ cup butter, chilled (1 stick)
- 1 shallot, finely minced (½ cup)
- 1 large clove garlic, finely minced or pressed (1 tsp.)
- ½ cup dry white wine (Sauvignon Blanc or Pinot Grigio)
- 3 Tbsp. white wine vinegar
- 4 Tbsp. heavy cream
- ¾ tsp. salt
- ¼ tsp. ground white or black pepper

MAKE AHEAD:
Beurre Blanc Deviled Eggs can be made one day before serving. Keep covered and refrigerated until serving time.

VEGETARIAN

Directions

1. **For eggs:** Peel eggs and cut them in half, top-to-bottom.
2. Remove cooked yolks and place them in a small mixing bowl. Mash yolks with a fork.
3. Arrange egg white halves, cut side up, on a serving plate or platter.
4. **For beurre blanc:** In a 1-quart saucepan over medium-high heat, melt 1 tablespoon butter.
5. Add shallots and garlic to pan. Cook, stirring occasionally, until shallots are translucent (about 5 minutes).
6. Add wine and vinegar to pan. Bring to a boil. Reduce heat to medium. Allow mixture to simmer until reduced to about ½ cup (15 minutes). Stir occasionally.
7. When sauce is reduced, add cream, salt, and pepper to pan. Bring to a low boil.
8. Cut the remaining butter into about 16 pieces. Add a piece or two of butter to the pot and stir until the butter is melted and incorporated. Repeat this process until all of the butter is incorporated.
9. Immediately remove pan from heat. Pour beurre blanc sauce over mashed yolks in bowl. Using a whisk, stir and mash the yolks until the sauce is incorporated. Allow yolk mixture to cool to room temperature.
10. Using a spoon or pastry bag fitted with a large star tip, fill yolk-holes in egg whites with the yolk mixture (mixture should be mounded up). Distribute filling evenly and use it all up. Serve deviled eggs immediately or cover and refrigerate.

GOUGÈRES

Makes 32 three-inch cream puffs

Gougères are a French cream puff, blessed with cheesy goodness. Simple ingredients, unforgettable results.

Ingredients

- 1 cup water
- ½ cup butter (1 stick)
- 1 ½ tsp. salt
- pinch sugar
- pinch ground white pepper
- 1 ½ cups all-purpose flour
- 4–5 large eggs
- 1 ¼ cups grated Gruyere cheese (5 oz.), divided

MAKE AHEAD:
Gougères can be made ahead through step #9 and frozen. Freeze the mounds of dough on the baking sheet, then transfer to a covered container or ziptop bag. Frozen Gougère dough will keep for 3 months. Transfer frozen dough back onto a baking sheet, allow to thaw, then bake. Gougères are best served freshly baked.

Directions

1. Preheat oven to 450°.
2. In a 2-quart saucepan, combine water, butter, salt, sugar, and pepper. Place pan over medium-high heat and bring to a boil. Stir occasionally.
3. Add flour and stir in.
4. Reduce heat to medium. Cook and stir mixture for two minutes, until mixture forms a ball of dough, and no flecks of white flour remain.
5. Remove pan from heat and continue stirring for about a minute to cool mixture slightly.
6. Add the eggs, one at a time. Work quickly and beat vigorously to incorporate each raw egg before it cooks and scrambles in the warm dough. Add four of the eggs and then re-assess. The finished dough should be smooth, silky, and stiff enough to form a peak with a tip that falls over. Test this by sticking a wooden spoon into the dough and lifting the spoon out—a peak of dough should form, then wilt.
7. If your dough is too stiff, add the last egg and beat in.
8. Add 1 cup grated cheese and mix in. Pipe or scoop batter onto greased baking sheets, in mounds of 1 tablespoon each (a ⅔ oz. cookie scoop works great for this). Place scoops 1" apart to allow for rising during baking.
9. Using the remaining ¼ cup of grated cheese, place a few gratings of cheese on top of each mound of dough.
10. Bake gougères for 7 minutes, then reduce heat to 350°. Bake an additional 20–25 minutes, until gougères are golden brown.
11. Transfer gougères to a serving plate or platter. Serve hot or at room temperature.

VEGETARIAN

CHEESE TART

Makes 36 appetizer squares

This tart is amazing! The creaminess of the cheese in combination with the salty pungency of the anchovies and sweetness of the onions is spectacular!

Ingredients

Onions:

- 2 Tbsp. butter or vegetable oil
- 3 large white or yellow onions, thinly sliced (5–6 cups)
- 2 large cloves garlic (2 tsp.), minced and smashed to a paste with ¼ tsp. salt

Cheese:

- ½ cup small curd cottage cheese
- 8 oz. shredded gruyere or smoked gruyere cheese (2 cups)

Crust:

- 16 oz. package puff pastry, thawed and chilled

Topping:

- two 2 oz. tins anchovies
- 1 tsp. dried tarragon or thyme

VEGETARIAN

Directions

1. **For onions:** In a large frying pan over medium heat, melt the butter. Swirl pan to coat the bottom. Add onions.
2. Reduce heat to low (3 on a scale of 1 to 10) and cover pan. Cook onions, stirring occasionally, for 30–45 minutes, until onions are greatly reduced in volume and beginning to caramelize. Add garlic about halfway through cooking time.
3. **For cheese:** In a small mixing bowl, combine the cottage and gruyere cheeses. Toss and stir gently to combine.
4. Preheat oven to 425°.
5. **To assemble:** Remove puff pastry from package and lay on a well-floured work surface. Unfold, sprinkle lightly with flour, and roll out slightly. If the package contains two sheets of puff pastry, overlap one edge of each to create one large sheet.
6. Transfer puff pastry to a greased, large baking sheet. Prick pastry all over with the tines of a fork to keep it from over-rising (pricks about 1" apart).
7. Bake pastry for 10 minutes. While pastry is baking, cut each anchovy in half lengthwise.
8. Remove pastry from oven. Working quickly, spread the onion mixture over the entire surface of the pastry, distributing all the way to the edges.
9. Sprinkle the cheese mixture over the onions (hands work great for this).
10. Lay anchovies on top of tart, spacing them out, and creating a decorative pattern.
11. Sprinkle thyme evenly over all.
12. Bake tart for 10 minutes more, until cheese is beginning to brown.
13. Cut tart into 36 pieces. Transfer to a serving platter and serve hot.

MAKE AHEAD:
The onions can be cooked up to 4 days ahead of assembly and baking of this dish. Keep them covered and refrigerated.

LOBSTER THERMIDORS

Makes 36 tartlets

These little pies are very rich, and the filling oh-so-very French. If you aren't able to find lobster meat in your area, you can substitute 8 ounces lump crab meat and then, of course, call them Crab Thermidors :~)

Ingredients

Filling:

- ½ cup dry white wine (Pinot Grigio or Sauvignon Blanc)
- 2 Tbsp. butter
- ½ cup finely minced shallot (1 shallot)
- 2 tsp. finely minced or pressed garlic (2 large cloves)
- 2 Tbsp. all-purpose flour
- ¾ cup heavy cream
- 2 large egg yolks
- ½ cup shredded Gruyere cheese (2 oz.)
- 1 tsp. dried parsley
- ½ tsp. dried tarragon or thyme
- ¾ tsp. salt
- ½ tsp. paprika (sweet or smoked)
- ¼ tsp. dry mustard powder
- ⅛ tsp. ground black pepper
- pinch cayenne pepper
- 7 oz. cooked lobster meat, diced (2 tails) or 2 cups langostino lobster tails (thaw if frozen)

Shells:

- 2 tubes refrigerated crescent dough sheet (8 oz. each)

Directions

1. **For filling:** In a small saucepan over medium heat, simmer wine until it is reduced to 2 tablespoons (about 15 minutes).
2. Place a separate 2-quart saucepan over medium-high heat. When pan is hot, add butter, shallot, and garlic. Sauté until shallot is translucent (about 2 minutes), stirring often.
3. Add flour to shallot pan. Stir until no white spots of flour remain. Cook 2 minutes more, stirring constantly.
4. In a small bowl, whisk cream and egg yolks together. Add mixture to shallot pan. Stir until mixture thickens and comes to a simmer (bubbles around edges of pan).
5. Add wine reduction, cheese, and spices to the pan. Stir until cheese is melted. Remove from heat, add lobster, and stir. Taste, and adjust seasonings as needed.
6. **To assemble:** Preheat oven to 375°.
7. On a lightly floured surface, unroll crescent dough sheets. With a rolling pin, gently roll each sheet out until 7 ½" x 15".
8. Cut each sheet of dough into 18 squares (2 ½" x 2 ½"). Place each square in the cup of a greased mini-muffin tin. Gently press dough down, to form a cup.
9. Bake cups for 5 minutes.
10. Remove cups from oven and quickly fill each cup with 1 tablespoon of the cooked lobster mixture. Use up all the filling and distribute it equally.
11. Return pans to oven and bake 10–15 minutes more.
12. Transfer finished tartlets to a serving platter (a soup spoon works great to lift the pies out of the tins). Garnish with a light sprinkling of minced fresh parsley or chives, if desired. Serve hot.

MAKE AHEAD:
The filling for Lobster Thermidors can be made 1 day ahead of assembly and baking. Keep filling covered and refrigerated.

SEAFOOD

GOING IT ALONE PARTY PREP COUNTDOWN

WEEKS BEFORE:
- Make Olive Tapenade with Feta and freeze
- Make Hummus and freeze
- Make Baklava Thumbprint Cookies and freeze
- Make Spanakopita and freeze

4 DAYS BEFORE:
- Make Skordalia
- Make Tzatziki
- Make Toum
- Make Honey-Lemon Dip

3 DAYS BEFORE:
- Make Mediterranean Tuna Salad (do not fill shells)

2 DAYS BEFORE:
- Mix and chill Falafel Fritter mix
- Roast vegetables and make sauce for Moussaka Tarts

1 DAY BEFORE:
- Fry Falafel Fritters
- Make Cod Fritters
- Make Shrimp Souvlaki
- Remove from freezer to thaw: Olive Tapenade, Hummus, Baklava Cookies, Spanakopita

DAY OF PARTY:
Morning
- Set up food table and choose platters, bowls, and trays for serving all dishes
- Prep fresh vegetables and refrigerate

2 Hours Before Party
- Assemble and bake Moussaka Tarts

1 Hour Before Party
- Bake Spanakopita
- Re-heat in oven: Cod Fritters, Falafel Fritters
- Assemble Mediterranean Tuna Salad Cups

GREECE

PARTY FOR 18

I must confess that my image of Greek cuisine has been forever influenced by the movie "My Big Fat Greek Wedding." The abundance, the communal preparation of complex dishes, the central place that food has in familial and community gatherings, plus the notion that you can unabashedly grill on your front lawn! I love all of that!

I also love how healthy Greek food is. Greece itself sits central in the Mediterranean Sea, and Greek cuisine is at the heart of a Mediterranean diet. Rich in antioxidants and anti-aging nutrients, my menu features a variety of traditional Greek dishes like Spanakopita and Shrimp Souvlaki, along with twists on the familiar like Moussaka Tarts and Baklava Cookies. If you are flying solo and making all the dishes in this chapter on your own, do so with confidence, as the most time-consuming dishes can be made well ahead of party time and frozen, leaving a manageable list for the final countdown.

HONEY-LEMON DIP WITH FRUIT

Makes 2 cups dip

When I finally had this dip recipe just right, I ate it by the spoonful straight out of the bowl. I wanted to, you know, make sure it was good. It was. It is. Great on fresh strawberries or dried fruit, it is a heavenly mix of creamy, sweet, and tart.

Ingredients

Dip:

- 8 oz. brick cream cheese, at room temperature
- 5 oz. carton plain Greek yogurt (½ cup)
- ½ cup honey
- zest and juice of 1 fresh lemon (2 tsp. zest + 4 Tbsp. juice, seeds strained out)
- ⅛ tsp. salt

Fruit:

- 1 ½ lbs. assorted dried fruit (apricots, strawberries, apples, and prunes are best and authentically Grecian) or 3 lbs. fresh strawberries

Directions

1. **For dip:** In a medium mixing bowl, combine cream cheese and yogurt. Beat with a whisk until smooth.
2. Add remaining ingredients. Stir dip until smooth.
3. Transfer dip to a serving bowl. Serve dip chilled or at room temperature with fruit on the side for dipping.

MAKE AHEAD:
Honey-Lemon Dip can be made up to 5 days ahead of serving. Keep covered and refrigerated.

HUMMUS WITH FRESH VEGETABLES

Makes 2 cups dip

There are nearly unlimited ways to make hummus, most all of which call for tahini to one degree or another. I dislike tahini, so I created this using peanut butter, to great success. It has a hint of heat from the chipotle pepper powder, and pairs wonderfully with raw vegetables or plain pita chips.

Ingredients

Dip:

- 14 oz. can chickpeas beans, drained and liquid reserved
- ¼ cup sliced green onions (1–2 onions) or diced red onion
- 3 large cloves garlic, sliced (1 Tbsp.)
- 3 Tbsp. natural peanut butter
- 2 Tbsp. olive oil
- 2 Tbsp. lemon juice
- 8 dashes Frank's Red Hot pepper sauce (or another sweet hot sauce)
- ¼ tsp. chipotle pepper powder
- ¼ tsp. ground cumin
- ¼ tsp. smoked sea salt or plain salt

Veggies:

- 1 lb. baby carrots or carrot sticks
- 1 cucumber, sliced (6"–8" cuke)
- 1 sweet red or yellow bell pepper, seeded and cut in ¼" strips
- 1 pint cherry tomatoes

Directions

1. In container of a food processor or blender, dump all ingredients for the dip plus ½ of the reserved liquid from the chickpeas.
2. Process until smooth.
3. Add more chickpea liquid if the mixture is too thick and dry, and pulse to incorporate.
4. Taste hummus and adjust seasonings.
5. Transfer hummus to a serving bowl. Serve hummus chilled or at room temperature with raw vegetables on the side for dipping.
6. **NOTE:** the remaining chickpea liquid can be stored in the refrigerator or freezer and used as a substitute for eggs (¼ cup = 1 egg) in vegan or low cholesterol baked goods.

MAKE AHEAD:
Hummus can be made up to 1 week ahead of serving if refrigerated, and up to 3 months ahead if frozen. Thaw and stir before serving.

SHRIMP SOUVLAKI

Makes 20 appetizer-sized skewers

I became hooked on Shrimp Souvlaki from my favorite Greek restaurant and needed to learn to make it for myself. As it is "just" grilled shrimp, I thought it would be easy-peasy, but no. It took SO MANY trials to get just the right balance of seasonings to pair with the delicate flavor of the shrimp. I still frequent "my" Greek restaurant, but love that I can make these at home anytime the craving strikes.

Ingredients

Skewers:
- 20 six-inch bamboo skewers

Shrimp:
- 2 lbs. shrimp, peeled and de-veined (tails on or off, your choice)
- 2 Tbsp. olive oil
- 2 Tbsp. lemon juice
- 2 tsp. dried oregano
- 2 tsp. dried parsley
- 1 tsp. dried dill weed
- 1 tsp. garlic powder
- ½ tsp. salt

Serving:
- 1 cup toum (store-bought or homemade from recipe on page 80)

MAKE AHEAD:
Shrimp Souvlaki can be made a day ahead of serving. Keep covered and refrigerated. Allow to warm to room temperature before serving.

Directions

1. **For skewers:** In a shallow dish or tall glass, set skewers to soak in water.
2. **For shrimp:** In a medium mixing bowl, combine all ingredients for shrimp. Stir well, to coat shrimp evenly. Allow shrimp to marinate in seasonings for at least 10 minutes, and up to 2 hours.
3. Thread shrimp on bamboo skewers, dividing shrimp evenly (2–3 shrimp per skewer, depending on size of shrimp).
4. Turn oven broiler on, to high setting. Move upper oven rack so that it is about 4" below broiler.
5. Lay shrimp skewers out on a baking sheet.
6. When broiler is hot, cook shrimp under broiler for about 3 minutes on each side. Shrimp will be pink, opaque, and firm to the touch when done.
7. Alternatively, shrimp may be cooked over medium coals on a charcoal grill.
8. Transfer shrimp souvlaki to a serving platter, accompanied by toum for dipping. Serve shrimp hot or at room temperature.

SEAFOOD

OLIVE TAPENADE WITH FETA

Makes 3 cups

This tapenade is deliciously versatile—straight out of the bowl, as a topping for burgers, as a condiment for sandwiches or wraps, or as a topping for a Greek pizza. And, unlike other tapenades, it is attractive and appetizing, making it party-perfect. Most recipes for tapenade have you process the mixture into a spreadable paste which looks like, well, dog food. With this recipe, you are instructed to exercise restraint with the food processor, so that what you get is beautiful diced olives in a rustic relish, with the colors of the different olives visible.

Ingredients

Tapenade:

- 6 oz. can pitted black olives, drained
- ½ cup green olives stuffed with red pepper (about 2 oz.), drained
- ¼ cup pitted kalamata olives (about 1 oz.), drained
- ¼ cup capers
- ¼ cup raisins
- 2 large green onions, cut in 1" pieces or ½ cup roughly chopped red onion
- 2 garlic cloves, sliced (if making this without a food processor, finely mince and smash the garlic into a paste)
- 1 Tbsp. dried parsley
- 1 tsp. dried basil
- 2 Tbsp. olive oil
- 2 Tbsp. balsamic vinegar
- 1 Tbsp. anchovy paste
- 1 tsp. brown mustard
- 1 tsp. lemon juice
- 4 oz. feta cheese, crumbled (1 cup)

Serving:

- 16 oz. package pita chips

Directions

1. In the bowl of a food processor fitted with a steel blade, dump all ingredients for the tapenade except the feta. Pulse 10–15 times, until the mixture is finely minced (1/16" to 1/8" pieces), but the colors of different olives remain distinct.
2. Transfer the olive mixture to a medium mixing bowl. Add the feta and gently fold in.
3. If you don't have access to a food processor, simply chop all of the solids (except feta) with a sharp knife until finely minced. Place in a medium mixing bowl, add the remaining ingredients, and stir.
4. Serve tapenade with pita chips on the side for scooping.

MAKE AHEAD:
Olive Tapenade with Feta can be made up to 4 days ahead of serving if refrigerated, and up to 3 months ahead if frozen. Thaw before serving.

MEDITERRANEAN TUNA SALAD CUPS

Makes 75 bite-sized tartlets

I love these! They are easy to make (look how short the instructions are!), the filling can be mixed up days ahead of time to avoid last-minute drama, and the finished tartlets assemble in minutes. They also happen to be pretty and really tasty!

Ingredients

Filling:

- three 5 oz. cans water packed tuna, drained and flaked
- 14 oz. can artichoke hearts, drained and finely chopped
- 6 oz. can black olives, drained and finely chopped
- ½ cup finely minced red onion or green onions (2–3 onions)
- 2 Tbsp. diced red bell pepper
- 1 Tbsp. capers
- 1 cup feta cheese, crumbled (4 oz.)
- 1 Tbsp. dried parsley
- 2 tsp. dried oregano
- 1 tsp. dried basil
- ¼ tsp salt
- ¼ tsp. ground black pepper
- 5 Tbsp. olive oil
- 4 Tbsp. red wine vinegar

Shells:

- five 1.9 oz. packages frozen mini phyllo pastry shells (15 shells per package, no need to thaw)

> **VARIATION:**
> Mediterranean Tuna Salad can also be served stuffed inside mini-pita breads. Cut the pitas in half and fill with salad.

Directions

1. **For filling:** In large mixing bowl, combine all ingredients for filling.
2. Gently stir mixture until everything is coated in oil and vinegar.
3. **To assemble:** Remove pastry shells from packaging and place shells on a serving platter.
4. Fill pastry shells with filling, mounding the filling up. Serve immediately.
5. Do not fill pastry shells more than 30 minutes ahead of serving time. The shells will begin to lose their crispiness the longer they sit with the moist filling inside.

MAKE AHEAD:
Mediterranean Tuna Salad can be made through step #2 up to 3 days ahead of serving. Keep covered and refrigerated.

BAKLAVA THUMBPRINT COOKIES

Makes 80 bite-sized cookies

These cookies capture the sticky, honey-sweet goodness of baklava, without the crumbly mess. Or the time-consuming preparation. More than "just a cookie," they are the perfect dessert to cap off an evening of delicious revelry.

Ingredients

Dough:

- 1 cup butter, at room temperature (2 sticks)
- ½ cup light brown sugar
- ½ cup honey
- 2 large egg yolks
- 1 tsp. vanilla extract
- 4 cups all-purpose flour
- ½ tsp. ground cinnamon
- ½ tsp. salt

Filling:

- 1 cup finely chopped walnuts (6 oz.)
- ½ cup honey
- ½ tsp. ground cinnamon
- ⅛ tsp. ground cardamom
- ½ tsp. vanilla extract

MAKE AHEAD:
Baklava Thumbprint Cookies can be made ahead and stored at room temperature for up to 3 days or frozen for up to 3 months. Thaw before serving.

Directions

1. **For dough:** In a large mixing bowl, cream butter and sugar together.
2. Add honey, egg yolks, and vanilla. Blend in.
3. Add remaining ingredients for dough. Mix until no white spots of flour remain. Dough will be stiff and mixing with hands may be necessary.
4. **For filling:** In a small mixing bowl, combine all ingredients for filling. Stir until thoroughly combined.
5. Preheat oven to 350°.
6. Roll dough into small, ½ tablespoon-sized balls (a small cookie scoop works great for this). Place balls 1" apart on greased baking sheets.
7. Create a deep, round depression in the center of each ball, using a fingertip or the handle of a wooden spoon. Doing this will flatten the balls slightly.
8. Fill each depression with ½ teaspoon of filling (filling should be mounded up a bit).
9. Bake cookies for 10 minutes. When done, the cookies will be a light golden brown and the filling will be bubbling. Transfer cookies to a cooling rack and allow to cool completely before serving.

COD FRITTERS WITH SKORDALIA

Makes 48 bite-sized pieces

These fish fritters are tender and tasty on their own, but a dip in garlicky skordalia makes them positively POW! WOWZERS! And very Greek!

Ingredients

Frying:
- 8 cups vegetable oil for deep frying (64 oz.)

Batter:
- 1 cup all-purpose flour
- 1 tsp. baking powder
- 1 tsp. salt
- 1 large egg
- 1 cup dry white wine (Pinot Grigio or Sauvignon Blanc) or pale beer

Dredging:
- ½ cup whole wheat flour

Fish:
- 2 lb. raw cod, cut in 1" chunks (raw calamari rings or raw shucked oysters may be substituted)

Serving:
- 1 cup Greek skordalia (store-bought or homemade from recipe on page 80)

Directions

1. If making homemade skordalia, do that first.
2. **For frying:** In a stockpot, deep frying pan, electric fryer, or wok, heat oil to 350° (a deep-fry thermometer is invaluable). Oil should be at least 3" deep. Line a baking sheet with several layers of paper towels or newspaper, lay a cooling rack upside down on top of paper, and set aside.
3. **For batter:** In a small mixing bowl, combine flour, baking powder, and salt. Mix well.
4. Add egg and wine. Stir with a whisk until batter is pretty smooth (small lumps are fine).
5. **For dredging:** In a gallon-sized ziptop bag, place the flour. Drop about one-quarter of the chunks of cod into the bag. Seal the bag and shake to coat the fish pieces in flour.
6. When oil is up to temperature, remove fish pieces from the bag, dip them in batter, and drop them into the oil. Batter and fry as many pieces as will fit in a single layer, being careful to not over-crowd the oil. Dredge, batter, and cook the fish in batches as needed.
7. Fry fish for 3–4 minutes, flipping pieces as needed for even browning.
8. Remove fish with tongs or a kitchen spider and place on prepared tray to drain.
9. Allow oil to come back up to temperature before frying the next batch of fish.
10. Transfer cooked fish to a serving platter, accompanied by a bowl of skordalia for dipping. Serve fish hot.
11. **NOTE:** If you have batter leftover, it makes excellent onion rings.

MAKE AHEAD:
Cod Fritters can be made a day before serving. Keep covered and refrigerated. Re-heat fish on a baking sheet in a 300° oven for 10 minutes.

TOUM
Makes 1 cup

Toum is a versatile, mayonnaise-like sauce of Mediterranean origins. A classic to accompany souvlaki, it is also tasty on falafel.

Ingredients
- 3 large cloves garlic (1 Tbsp.), finely minced and smashed into a paste with ½ tsp. salt
- ⅓ cup plain Greek yogurt or sour cream
- 1 Tbsp. lemon juice
- 1 Tbsp. cold water
- ½ cup canola oil

Directions
1. Place garlic, yogurt, lemon juice, and water in a mug or small bowl. Whisk until smooth.
2. Add the oil. Whisk vigorously until mixture is emulsified.
3. Transfer toum to a covered container and refrigerate until needed. Toum will keep for one month.

TZATZIKI SAUCE
Makes 1 ½ cups

The tang of yogurt plus the bite of garlic balanced by the coolness of cucumber makes tzatziki one of the greatest condiments ever invented. Fantastic on all things Mediterranean.

Ingredients
- 1 cup plain Greek yogurt
- 1 cup cucumber, peeled, grated, and drained (put in a strainer and press the moisture out)
- 1 large clove garlic (1 tsp.), finely minced and smashed to a paste with ½ tsp. salt
- ⅛ tsp. black pepper
- pinch of sugar
- 1 Tbsp. olive oil
- 1 Tbsp. white wine vinegar

Directions
1. In a small bowl, combine all ingredients. Whisk until emulsified.
2. Transfer tzatziki to a covered container and refrigerate at least 1 hour before serving. Tzatziki will keep for 2 weeks.

SKORDALIA
Makes 2 cups

Skordalia is a Greek dipping sauce made from mashed potatoes and what appears at first glance to be Way Too Much Garlic. Not to worry, it is a wonderful, balanced, garlicky-but-not-overwhelmingly-so companion for fried foods, most especially fried fish.

Ingredients
- 6 large cloves garlic (2 Tbsp.)
- 4 Tbsp. lemon juice
- 2 Tbsp. white wine vinegar
- 14 oz. can potatoes, drained
- ½ cup olive oil
- 1 Tbsp. dried parsley
- 1 Tbsp. dried chives
- ½ tsp. salt

Directions
1. In the container of a blender, add garlic, lemon juice, and vinegar. Process on high until mixture is smooth (blending garlic with an acid eliminates bitterness).
2. Add remaining ingredients. Process on high until smooth.
3. Transfer skordalia to a covered container and refrigerate until needed. Skordalia will keep for two weeks.

FALAFEL FRITTERS

Makes 64 appetizer triangles

These are such tasty triangles of joy! Firmer and less crumbly than traditional falafel, they are a true finger food. To keep them vegan, serve them with a vegan Greek yogurt.

Ingredients

Fritters:

- 15 oz can chickpeas, drained (reserve liquid) and roughly chopped
- chickpea liquid + vegetable broth or water to make 4 cups
- 12 oz. box dried falafel mix (2 ½ cups dry mix)
- 1 cup instant corn Masa flour (for making tortillas) or cornmeal
- 1 Tbsp. dried parsley

Frying:

- 8 cups vegetable oil for deep-frying (64 oz.)

Serving:

- 1 cup tzatziki sauce (store-bought or homemade from recipe on opposite page) or plain Greek yogurt

Directions

1. **For fritters:** Grease a 9" x 13" baking pan and set aside.
2. In a 2-quart saucepan over medium-high heat, bring liquids to a boil.
3. Reduce heat to medium-low and add remaining ingredients.
4. Stir vigorously until no lumps remain (about 1 minute) and remove from heat.
5. Spread mixture in prepared pan.
6. Lightly oil your hand. Pat mixture to compress it and to spread it to an even thickness.
7. Cover pan. Refrigerate mixture at least 2 hours, and preferably overnight.
8. **For frying:** In a stockpot, deep frying pan, electric fryer, or wok, heat oil to 375° (a deep-fry thermometer is invaluable). Oil should be at least 3" deep. Line a baking sheet with several layers of paper towels or newspaper, lay a cooling rack upside down on top of paper, and set aside.
9. Cut chilled fritter mixture into 64 triangles (32 squares cut in half; cut pan into 8 columns x 4 rows for squares).
10. When oil is up to temperature, drop triangles into oil in batches (don't crowd pan or triangles will stick together and cook unevenly). Cook each batch for about 3 minutes, flipping over as needed for even browning.
11. Remove triangles with a kitchen spider and place on prepared tray to drain.
12. Allow oil to return to 375° before adding the next batch of triangles.
13. Transfer fritters to a serving platter. Serve warm with tzatziki sauce on the side for dipping.

MAKE AHEAD:
Falafel Fritters can be made up to 2 days before serving. Keep covered and refrigerated. Re-heat fritters on a baking sheet in a 300° oven for 10 minutes.

MOUSSAKA TARTS

Makes 24

Traditional moussaka is like an eggplant lasagna—definitely not something to be eaten with your hands. These tarts, however, pack all that yummy moussaka goodness into a neat pastry cup, perfect to pick up and enjoy. And if you can find a package of vegan puff pastry to substitute, you can make these vegan.

― Ingredients ―

Eggplant:

- 1 large eggplant
- 1 head garlic
- ½ tsp. olive oil
- ¼ tsp. salt

Sauce:

- 12 oz. package soy crumbles
- 14 oz. can tomato sauce or puree (not pasta sauce)
- ½ cup finely minced red onion (half of a medium onion)
- 4 large cloves garlic, finely minced or pressed (4 tsp.)
- ¼ cup dry red wine (Cabernet Sauvignon or Merlot)
- 2 Tbsp. tomato paste
- 1 Tbsp. dried parsley
- 2 tsp. dried oregano
- ½ tsp. ground cinnamon
- ½ tsp. salt
- ⅛ tsp. ground black pepper
- ⅛ tsp. red pepper flakes

Shells:

- 16 oz. package puff pastry, thawed and chilled

Directions

1. **For eggplant:** Preheat oven to 425°.
2. Cut off stem end of eggplant. Cut eggplant in half, top to bottom. Lay halves, cut side down, on a greased baking sheet.
3. Cut head of garlic in half horizontally. Lay bottom half on a square of aluminum foil. Drizzle oil over cut side. Replace top half of garlic head. Pull foil up and around garlic, sealing packet shut. Lay wrapped garlic on baking sheet with eggplant.
4. Roast vegetables in oven for 45 minutes.
5. Scoop cooked eggplant flesh into a colander and allow to drain. Transfer drained eggplant to a small mixing bowl.
6. Pop the roasted garlic cloves out of their papery coverings and add to the eggplant. Use a potato masher or a fork to mash the eggplant and garlic into chunky bits. Add salt to eggplant and mix in. Set aside.
7. **For sauce:** In a large mixing bowl, combine all ingredients for sauce. Stir well.
8. **To assemble:** Preheat oven to 400°.
9. Remove puff pastry from package and unfold onto a generously floured work surface.
10. With a rolling pin, gently roll pastry out to an even thickness, enlarging the dough (whether one sheet or two) so that you can cut 24 equal-sized squares out of it, each about 3 ½" square (6 columns x 4 rows). Cut dough into 24 squares.
11. Lightly grease two regular-sized muffin tins.
12. Place one square of puff pastry in each cup of the muffin tins. Gently press pastry in, to form a cup.
13. Prick each pastry cup bottom three times with the tines of a fork (this keeps the pastry from over-inflating).
14. Bake pastry cups for 5 minutes.
15. Remove cups from oven and quickly place ½ tablespoon of the eggplant mixture in the bottom of each cup. Use up all the eggplant and distribute equally.
16. Quickly top the eggplant with 1 ½ tablespoons of sauce per cup. Use up all of the sauce and distribute equally.
17. Return tarts to oven and bake 15–20 minutes more, until pastry is lightly browned.
18. Transfer finished tarts to a serving platter (a soup spoon works great to lift the pies out of the tins). Garnish with a few pinches of chopped parsley, if desired. Serve hot.

MAKE AHEAD:
The eggplant and sauce for Moussaka Tarts can be prepared up to 3 days ahead of assembly and baking. Keep them separate and refrigerated.

SPANAKOPITA (SPINACH PIES)

Makes 36 appetizer-sized pies

The first time you make these, allow yourself extra time. Working with phyllo pastry is a delicate business, and does not go well when rushed. Once you get the hang of it, the process of making these will go faster, but it will take one whole batch to get you there.

--- Ingredients ---

Filling:

- three 16 oz. packages frozen, chopped spinach (or five 10 oz. packages), thawed and drained
- 6 large eggs
- ¾ cup thinly sliced green onions (6–8 onions)
- 1 Tbsp. finely minced or pressed garlic (3 large cloves)
- 3 Tbsp. dried parsley
- 2 Tbsp. dried dill weed
- 1 tsp. salt
- ¼ tsp. ground nutmeg
- 2 tsp. lemon juice
- 16 oz. diced or crumbled feta cheese (3–4 cups, depending on size of pieces)

Wrappers:

- 16 oz. package phyllo pastry sheets, thawed if frozen (9" x 14" sheets)
- 1 cup melted butter (2 sticks)

84　PARTY ON!

Directions

1. **For filling:** In a large mixing bowl, combine all filling ingredients except feta cheese. Stir well to thoroughly blend ingredients.
2. Add feta and gently fold in.
3. **To assemble:** Open package of phyllo. Lay sheets of pastry out flat, between two pieces of kitchen parchment or plastic. Cover top parchment with a damp towel.
4. Fold back covering and remove one thin sheet of phyllo. Lay this sheet out flat on a clean work surface.
5. Brush melted butter over the surface of the sheet of phyllo, and top with another sheet of phyllo.
6. Brush second sheet with melted butter, add a third sheet to the stack, brush with butter, and top with a fourth sheet.
7. Replace covering on remaining unused sheets of phyllo.
8. Cut the buttered stack of sheets into four strips, crosswise (each strip should be about 3 ½" x 9").
9. On one end of each strip, place 2 tablespoons filling.
10. Fold the end of one strip on the diagonal over the filling, forming the filling into a triangular shape.
11. Continue folding the strip up like a folded flag, until you have a triangular spinach pie with the filling tucked neatly inside.
12. Brush melted butter on bottom of spanakopita. Place pie on a baking sheet and brush top with butter.
13. Repeat process with remaining pastry and filling.
14. Preheat oven to 350°.
15. Bake pies for 25 minutes. Transfer spanakopita to a serving platter and serve hot.

MAKE AHEAD:
Spanakopita can be made through step #13 and frozen for up to 6 months ahead of baking and serving. Place baking sheet full of buttered pies in freezer. After pies are frozen hard, transfer them to an airtight container. Spanakopita do not need to be thawed before baking, and will bake in approximately the same amount of time.

VARIATION:
Spanakopita can be made in a larger, entree size. Butter and stack the phyllo sheets as instructed, but cut the stack into two strips (not four), lengthwise (not cross-wise). Place ⅓ cup filling on one end of each strip, and fold into a triangular pie, as instructed above. Larger spanikopita bake at the same oven temperature and in the same amount of time as the smaller, appetizer-sized pies.

GOING IT ALONE PARTY PREP COUNTDOWN

WEEKS BEFORE:
- ❏ Make Dal Dip and freeze
- ❏ Make Indian Peanut Dip and freeze
- ❏ Make Korma sauce for Korma Tofu and freeze
- ❏ Make Fish Pakoras and freeze
- ❏ Make Palak Paneer and freeze
- ❏ Make Samosas and freeze

4 DAYS BEFORE:
- ❏ Make Apricot Chutney
- ❏ Make Spiced Cashews

1 DAY BEFORE:
- ❏ Make Mango Cupcakes
- ❏ Remove from freezer to thaw: Dal Dip, Indian Peanut Dip, Korma sauce, Palak Paneer, Fish Pakoras, Samosas

DAY OF PARTY:
Morning
- ❏ Set tofu to drain
- ❏ Set up food table and choose platters, bowls, and trays for serving all dishes
- ❏ Prep fresh vegetables and refrigerate

90 Minutes Before Party
- ❏ Bake tofu for Korma Tofu, re-heat sauce, combine

45 Minutes Before Party
- ❏ Make Curried Shrimp
- ❏ Re-heat in oven: Palak Paneer, Fish Pakoras, Samosas

INDIA

PARTY FOR 18

I am happy to report that this chapter is the easiest of all the chapters to manage on your own. If you are flying solo in throwing a party, want to impress your guests, and are committed to single-handedly making a full finger food buffet, this is the chapter for you. All but three of the dishes here can be made well ahead of time and stashed in the freezer, leaving you with an extremely manageable to-do list in the days leading up to your party. This party is also fun to host, with guests getting into mixing-and-matching where the dips are concerned. In the recipes, I have paired the Indian Peanut Dip with fresh vegetables, the Dal Dip (lentil dip) with naan chips, and the Apricot Chutney with the Samosas and Fish Pakoras. But, truth be told, I like the Palak Paneer dipped in the Peanut Dip, vegetables dipped in the Apricot Chutney, and pretty much everything dipped in the Dal Dip.

Indian cuisine is among the most complex in the world because of the spice blends it employs. Please don't be put off by the length of ingredient lists, because most of each list will be handled by standing in front of your spice rack, scooping this and that into a bowl. Indian dishes are also known for their intense heat, and there is some of that here to dazzle the taste buds, with notations in ingredients lists for how to dial that up or down as desired.

SPICED CASHEWS

Makes 4 cups

The buttery nature of cashews works as a delicious foil for the gentle heat in the spices used here. Crunchy, salty, spicy, with an indescribable appeal, these are a favorite snack at my house!

Ingredients

Spice Blend:

- 1 Tbsp. chickpea flour or gluten-free flour mix
- 2 tsp. garam masala (store-bought or from recipe below)
- 1 tsp. chili powder (up to 3 tsp. for more intense heat)
- 1 tsp. ground ginger
- 1 tsp. salt
- ½ tsp. cardamom

Nuts:

- 4 cups roasted, salted whole cashews (18 oz.)
- 2 Tbsp. peanut or vegetable oil

MAKE AHEAD:
Spiced Cashews can be made up to a week before serving. Keep tightly covered at room temperature.

Garam Masala:

- 1 Tbsp. coriander
- 1 Tbsp. cardamom
- 2 tsp. cumin
- 2 tsp. ground cinnamon
- 1 tsp. black pepper

Mix spices together in a covered spice jar or airtight container. Store at room temperature.

Directions

1. Preheat oven to 350°.
2. In a mug or ramekin, combine ingredients for spice blend. Mix well.
3. Place cashews in a colander and quickly rinse in cold water. Shake excess water off, but do not dry cashews.
4. Transfer cashews to a medium mixing bowl. Add oil and stir to coat nuts.
5. Add spices to nuts. Stir until the spices are evenly distributed and no longer dry.
6. Transfer nuts to a greased baking sheet.
7. Bake for 15 minutes, stirring nuts once or twice during baking. Taste a nut to be sure they are crunchy. If not crunchy, bake a few minutes longer.
8. Remove nuts from oven and allow to cool. Transfer cashews to a serving bowl or airtight container.

VEGAN

DAL DIP WITH NAAN CHIPS
Makes 4 cups dip

This lentil dip is a lot like hummus in the texture of the finished dip, and the simplicity of its preparation. Spicy and full-flavored, I have made this as our contribution to several potluck parties we've been invited to, and people go absolutely nuts over it. I have yet to come home with more than a few tablespoons of this dip leftover, even after parties that feature way too much good food.

Ingredients

Dip:

- 14 oz. can lentils (do not drain)
- 6 oz. can tomato paste
- 4 oz. jar diced mild green chile peppers
- 5 oz. carton plain Greek yogurt (½ cup; use vegan yogurt to make this vegan)
- 1 red, orange, or yellow bell pepper, seeded and roughly chopped
- 1 cup sliced green onions (4–6 onions) or ½ cup chopped red onion
- 1 jalapeño pepper, with seeds
- 2 large cloves garlic (2 tsp.)
- 1 Tbsp. olive oil
- 1 Tbsp. lime juice (½ lime)
- 1 Tbsp. garam masala (store-bought or homemade from recipe on page 89)
- 1 ½ tsp. salt
- 1 tsp. ground ginger
- 1 tsp. ground coriander
- 1 tsp. chili powder
- ½ tsp. ground turmeric
- ¼ tsp. ground black pepper

Serving:

- 12 oz. bag naan chips or pita chips

Directions

1. **For dip:** In the container of a blender or food processor fitted with a steel blade, combine all dip ingredients.
2. Process on high until smooth. Taste, and adjust seasonings.
3. Transfer dip to a serving bowl. Serve with naan or pita chips on the side for scooping. Cover and refrigerate dip if not serving right away.

MAKE AHEAD:
Dal Dip can be made up to 1 week ahead of serving if refrigerated, and up to 3 months ahead if frozen. Thaw and stir before serving.

INDIAN PEANUT DIP WITH FRESH VEGETABLES

Makes 4 ½ cups dip

This protein-rich vegan dip is a winner! Full-flavored and quick to prepare, it is a great companion for a wide variety of foods. Add it to just about any finger food buffet and people will dip practically everything in it!

Ingredients

Dip:

- 16 oz. jar natural peanut butter (1 ½ cups)
- 14 oz. can coconut milk (1 ½ cups; regular, not lite)
- 4 oz. can mild, diced green chile peppers
- ¼ cup soy sauce
- ¼ cup fresh lime juice (2 limes)
- 3 Tbsp. maple syrup
- 2 Tbsp. rice wine vinegar
- 1 heaping Tbsp. finely minced or pressed garlic (4 large cloves)
- 1 Tbsp. ground ginger
- 2 tsp. garam masala (store-bought or from recipe on page 89)
- 1 tsp. ground turmeric
- 1 tsp. ground coriander
- 1 tsp. ground celery seed
- ½ tsp. ground cumin
- ½ tsp. red pepper flakes (increase to 1 tsp. for intense heat)
- ½ tsp. salt
- ¼ tsp. ground cinnamon
- ⅛ tsp. ground cloves

Veggies:

- 1 lb. baby carrots or carrot sticks
- 8 oz. package fresh peapods, strings removed
- 1 cucumber, sliced

Directions

1. In 2-quart saucepan, combine all ingredients for dip.
2. Place pan over medium heat and cook, stirring constantly, until dip is warmed, emulsified, and smooth. Do not allow mixture to boil or dip will separate (if dip separates, remove it from heat immediately and stir in 2–3 Tbsp. peanut butter).
3. Remove from heat and allow dip to cool. Transfer to a serving bowl surrounded by fresh vegetables for dipping.

MAKE AHEAD:
Indian Peanut Dip can be made up to 1 week ahead of serving if refrigerated, and up to 3 months ahead if frozen. Thaw and stir before serving.

CURRIED SHRIMP
Makes 4 cups

Traditional Indian curries include ground fenugreek in the spice blend. Fenugreek has a number of health benefits, but it also wreaks havoc with the blood sugars of diabetics. As my husband is in that camp, I have replaced the fenugreek here with celery and maple syrup. Traditional curries also feature a sauce, which is not needed here, thus making these shrimp the perfect finger food.

Ingredients

Curry Powder:

- 2 tsp. onion powder (bust up any lumps)
- 2 tsp. ground turmeric
- 1 tsp. ground celery seed
- ½ tsp. garam masala
- ½ tsp. ground ginger
- ½ tsp. salt
- ¼ tsp. garlic powder
- ¼ tsp. chili powder
- ⅛ tsp. cayenne pepper (for mild heat; increase up to 1 tsp. for intense heat)
- ⅛ tsp. ground black pepper

Shrimp:

- 2 lb. raw tail-on, peeled, de-veined shrimp (any size), patted dry
- 2 Tbsp. maple syrup
- 2 Tbsp. vegetable oil

Directions

1. Preheat oven broiler to LOW setting. Move oven rack to top position.
2. **For curry powder:** In ramekin or mug, combine all ingredients for curry powder. Stir well.
3. **For shrimp:** Place shrimp in a medium mixing bowl.
4. Add maple syrup and oil to shrimp. Stir until shrimp are coated.
5. Add curry powder to shrimp. Stir until shrimp are evenly covered and seasonings are moist.
6. Transfer shrimp to a greased baking sheet and spread out to a single layer.
7. Broil shrimp for 5 minutes.
8. Flip shrimp over and broil for 5 minutes more. Shrimp should be pink, opaque, and firm to the touch. Don't overcook shrimp or they will be become tough and rubbery.
9. Transfer shrimp to a serving bowl and serve.

SEAFOOD

FISH PAKORAS (FRITTERS)

Makes 40 fritters

Fish Pakoras are usually just cubed fish dipped in a thin coating of spicy batter and fried, while Vegetable Pakoras are a combination of onions, potatoes, and spices integrated into batter and fried. Mine are a delicious fusion of the two. These are fun to fry up and eat, as the batter is loose and the onions are rather mischievous. If done properly, the finished pakoras will resemble the nests of blind birds.

Ingredients

Frying:

- 8 cups vegetable oil for deep frying (64 oz.)

Batter:

- 1 lb. whitefish filets (cod, flounder, tilapia, or other), patted dry and cut in ½" dice
- 1 large white or yellow onion, peeled and cut top to bottom in ⅛" thick wedges (about 1 ½ cups)
- 1 fist-sized potato, peeled and grated (about 1 ½ cups)
- 4 oz. can mild, diced green chile peppers
- 2 Tbsp. grated fresh ginger root (peel and grate on a microplane or the superfine side of a box grater) or 1 Tbsp. dried ginger
- 1 Tbsp. finely minced or pressed garlic (3 large cloves)
- 1 Tbsp. finely minced fresh cilantro
- 1 ½ cups chickpea flour (if unavailable, substitute a gluten-free flour blend)
- 2 tsp. garam masala (store-bought or from recipe on page 89)
- 2 tsp. chili powder
- 1 tsp. salt
- ½ tsp. baking powder
- ½ tsp. ground turmeric
- 2 large eggs
- ¾ cup water

Directions

1. **For frying:** In a stockpot, deep frying pan, electric fryer, or wok, heat oil to 350° (a deep-fry thermometer is invaluable). Oil should be at least 3" deep. Line a baking sheet with several layers of paper towels or newspaper, lay a cooling rack upside down on top of paper, and set aside.
2. **For batter:** In a large mixing bowl, combine all batter ingredients except eggs and water. Stir to thoroughly combine and to coat everything in flour and spices.
3. Add eggs and water. Stir until batter mixture is evenly moist.
4. When oil is up to temperature, drop heaping tablespoon scoops of batter into oil. Do not crowd the pot—cook the pakoras in batches as needed. Cook each batch for 3–4 minutes total, flipping them over as needed for even browning. Some onion pieces or small bits may separate from the fritters. Keep them in the mix, as they make for fun noshing.
5. Remove pakoras from oil with a kitchen spider, and place on prepared tray. Allow oil to come back to temperature before adding next batch.
6. Transfer fish pakoras to a bowl or platter and serve hot.

MAKE AHEAD:
Fish Pakoras can be made up to 3 days ahead of serving if refrigerated, and up to 3 months ahead if frozen. Thaw and re-heat on a baking sheet in a 300° oven for 10 minutes.

APRICOT CHUTNEY

Makes 2 cups

This chutney is intense but not spicy, and works as a topping or dipping sauce for a wide variety of Indian dishes. If you are making this whole chapter, it is fantastic on the samosas and the fish pakoras.

Ingredients

Fennel:

- 1 bulb fennel
- 1 Tbsp. vegetable oil
- 1 Tbsp. balsamic vinegar
- ¼ tsp. salt

Chutney:

- ½ cup dried apricots (4 oz.)
- ½ cup raisins (standard or golden)
- 1 ¼ cups boiling water
- 1 Tbsp. grated fresh ginger root (peel and grate on a microplane or the super-fine side of a box grater) or 2 tsp. ground ginger
- 1 Tbsp. fresh cilantro leaves and small stems
- 2 tsp. honey
- ½ tsp. salt
- ½ tsp. chili powder
- ½ tsp. garam masala
- ½ tsp. ground coriander
- ¼ tsp. ground cardamom
- ⅛ tsp. dry mustard

Directions

1. **For fennel:** Preheat oven to 400°.
2. Cut top and root ends off fennel bulb. Remove any damaged spots. Cut bulb in half top-to-bottom and then in thin wedges.
3. In an 8" square baking pan, combine fennel, oil, vinegar, and salt. Mix together until fennel is coated in oil.
4. Roast fennel for 40 minutes. Stir once or twice during roasting. Continue with recipe while fennel roasts.
5. **For chutney:** Dice the apricots. Transfer apricots and raisins to a small mixing bowl and add the boiling water. Cover with a plate. Allow mixture to sit and absorb.
6. When fennel is done and fruit is hydrated, place all ingredients in a blender or food processor fitted with a steel blade (including any water with the fruit). Process on high until you have a chunky paste.
7. Transfer chutney to a serving bowl and serve.

MAKE AHEAD:
Apricot Chutney can be made up to a week before serving. Keep covered and refrigerated.

MANGO CUPCAKES

Makes 18 cupcakes

I wasn't sure my mango cake idea was going to work, as mango is such a juicy fruit, and more well-suited to making pies or custards. Undaunted, my first attempt worked out well enough that I pressed on. More cupcakes than I care to mention later, I had something fantastic. Moist, mango-y, with a nice cake-y crumb, these cupcakes are a true taste sensation!

Ingredients

Cake:

- 16 oz. bag frozen mango cubes, thawed, or flesh from 3 fresh mangoes (2 ½–3 cups)
- ½ cup light brown sugar
- ¼ cup plain Greek yogurt
- ¼ cup vegetable oil
- 3 large eggs
- 1 tsp. lemon juice
- 2 cups all-purpose flour
- ¼ cup cornstarch
- 1 tsp. ground cardamom
- 1 tsp. ground cinnamon
- 1 tsp. ground ginger
- 1 tsp. baking powder
- 1 tsp. baking soda
- ¼ tsp. salt

Frosting:

- ½ cup butter, at room temperature (1 stick)
- 4 oz. container mango baby food (½ cup)
- ½ tsp. vanilla extract
- 3 cups confectioner's sugar, sifted
- ⅛ tsp. salt

MAKE AHEAD:
Mango Cupcakes can be made 1 day ahead of serving if kept at room temperature or 2 days ahead if refrigerated.

Directions

1. Line two standard muffin tins with paper liners (18 cups in all). Set aside.
2. Preheat oven to 350°.
3. **For cake:** In the container of a blender, combine mango, sugar, yogurt, oil, eggs, and lemon juice. Process on high until smooth.
4. In a large mixing bowl, combine remaining dry ingredients for cake. Stir to combine.
5. Add blended wet ingredients to dry ingredients in bowl. Mix with a whisk just until combined and smooth.
6. Scoop batter into prepared muffin tins, distributing batter evenly and using it all up.
7. Bake cupcakes for 20 minutes. When done, cake will spring back when touched and a testing pick will come out clean.
8. Transfer cupcakes to a cooling rack. Allow to cool completely before frosting.
9. **For frosting:** In a large mixing bowl, combine butter, mango baby food, vanilla and ½ cup confectioner's sugar. With a hand mixer or whisk, beat until smooth.
10. Add remaining confectioner's sugar to bowl, one cup at a time. Beat after each addition. Add salt with last installment of sugar.
11. With a butter knife, spreader, or pastry bag fitted with a decorative tip, apply frosting to tops of cupcakes. These cupcakes can sit at room temperature for 1 day, but must be refrigerated after that.

VEGETARIAN

PALAK PANEER (CHEESE STICKS)

Makes 32 appetizers

You can certainly substitute Indian paneer for the mozzarella in this recipe. First, though, you will need to cut the paneer into sticks, lightly salt it, and pan-fry it in a bit of olive oil, before wrapping it in dough. This will firm up the cheese and enhance its flavor.

---- Ingredients ----

Dough:

- 15 oz. can potatoes (drained); or 2 fist-sized potatoes, cooked and peeled (bake, boil, or microwave); or 1 ½ cups leftover mashed potatoes
- 10 oz. package frozen, chopped spinach, thawed (do not drain)
- 4 oz. can mild, diced green chile peppers
- 1 cup coarsely chopped white or yellow onion (1 medium onion)
- 3 Tbsp. fresh cilantro leaves
- 3 large cloves garlic (1 Tbsp.)
- 3 quarter-sized slices peeled, fresh ginger or 2 tsp. ground ginger
- 1 large egg
- 1 cup chickpea flour or masa corn flour (as for tortillas)
- 1 cup plain bread crumbs
- 1 Tbsp. garam masala (store-bought or from recipe on page 89)
- 1 tsp. chili powder
- 1 tsp. ground coriander
- ½ tsp. ground cumin
- ½ tsp. ground cinnamon
- ½ tsp. salt
- ¼ tsp. ground black pepper
- ¼ tsp. ground cayenne pepper

Cheese:

- 16 oz. package mozzarella string cheese (unwrapped)

Frying:

- 8 cups vegetable oil for deep frying (64 oz.)

Serving:

- 8 oz. jar tamarind chutney (1 cup), or apricot chutney from recipe on page 94
- 1 cup plain Greek yogurt

MAKE AHEAD:

Palak Paneer can be made up to 3 days ahead of serving if refrigerated, and up to 3 months ahead if frozen. Thaw and lay sticks out on a baking sheet. Re-heat in a 300° oven for 10 minutes.

VEGETARIAN

Directions

1. **For dough:** In the container of a blender, combine potatoes, spinach, onion, cilantro, garlic, ginger, and egg. Process on high until smooth.
2. In a medium mixing bowl, combine dry ingredients for dough.
3. Add contents of blender to bowl. Stir to combine. Mixture should be the consistency of cookie dough. If mixture is too wet and sticky, add another ¼ cup flour.
4. **For frying:** In a stockpot, deep frying pan, electric fryer, or wok, heat oil to 350° (a deep-fry thermometer is invaluable). Oil should be at least 3" deep. Line a baking sheet with several layers of paper towels or newspaper, lay a cooling rack upside down on top of paper, and set aside. While oil heats, assemble sticks.
5. **For sticks:** Cut each 4" stick of cheese in half, making two 2" pieces each.
6. Pinch off a 1 ½ tablespoon-sized piece of dough. Flatten it into a patty in the palm of your hand. Place one piece of cheese on top. Wrap dough around cheese, enclosing all sides of cheese, and shaping the roll into a log. Set this aside. Repeat process with remaining dough and cheese.
7. When oil is up to temperature, drop cheese sticks into the pot. Do not crowd the pot—cook the sticks in batches as needed. Cook each batch for 3–4 minutes total, flipping them over as needed for even browning.
8. Remove sticks from oil with tongs or a kitchen spider and place on prepared tray. Allow oil to come back to temperature before adding next batch of sticks.
9. Transfer palak paneer to a serving bowl or platter. Serve hot with chutney and/or yogurt on the side for dipping.

KORMA TOFU
Makes 6 cups

Boring tofu, you ask? Heavens, no! This preparation yields crispy tofu cubes drenched in a sauce so spicy it's almost too much, but also so incredibly delicious that your guests will come back to this bowl again and again.

--- Ingredients ---

Tofu:

- three 14 oz. packages extra-firm tofu, drained
- 3 Tbsp. soy sauce
- 3 Tbsp. peanut or vegetable oil
- 3 Tbsp. cornstarch

Spice Blend:

- 2 Tbsp. ground coriander
- 1 tsp. ground cumin
- 1 tsp. garam masala (store-bought or from recipe on page 89)
- 1 tsp. salt
- ½ tsp. ground black pepper
- ¼ tsp. cayenne pepper
- ¼ tsp. ground turmeric

Sauce:

- 2 Tbsp. vegetable oil
- 1 cup finely minced white or yellow onion (1 medium onion)
- 1 Tbsp. finely minced or pressed garlic (3 large cloves)
- 1 Tbsp. grated fresh ginger root (peel and grate on a microplane or the super-fine side of a box grater) or 2 tsp. ground ginger
- ½ jalapeño pepper, seeds in, finely minced (use whole pepper for intense heat)
- 15 oz. can tomato sauce (plain; not pasta sauce)
- ¼ cup unsweetened shredded coconut
- ¼ cup plain Greek yogurt
- ¼ cup peanut butter
- 3 Tbsp. minced fresh cilantro
- 1 Tbsp. lemon juice

Directions

1. **For tofu:** Cut each block of tofu horizontally into three 4" x 6" slabs. Lay slabs out flat on several layers of paper towel or a folded tea towel, and top with more paper towels or another tea towel.
2. Place a baking sheet or cutting board on top of the tofu, and weigh it down (cans of food work great). Let sit at least 30 minutes, to press excess moisture out of the tofu.
3. Preheat oven to 400°.
4. Cut tofu slabs into 9 pieces each (3 rows x 3 columns). Transfer pieces to a large mixing bowl. Add soy sauce and oil. Using a rubber spatula, gently stir to coat tofu.
5. Add cornstarch. Gently stir until tofu is coated and no white spots of cornstarch remain. (Don't add the soy sauce, oil, and cornstarch all at once—it will make a gloppy mess.)
6. Transfer tofu to a large, greased baking sheet, laying the cubes in a single layer.
7. Bake tofu for 30–45 minutes, flipping pieces over in the middle of baking time (tofu should be lightly browned on both sides). While tofu is baking, prepare sauce.
8. **For sauce:** Measure all the ingredients for the spice blend into a ramekin or mug and set next to the cooktop.
9. Place a large frying pan over medium-high heat. Add the oil. When oil is hot, add the onions. Sauté until onions begin to brown (about 10 minutes).
10. Add the garlic, ginger, jalapeño, and spice blend. Cook for 1 minute, stirring constantly.
11. Add the remaining sauce ingredients. Stir, cover, reduce heat to low, and simmer for 10 minutes. Stir occasionally.
12. Turn burner off, but leave pan in place to stay warm.
13. Add baked tofu to sauce. Stir gently to coat tofu in sauce. Transfer tofu to a serving bowl. Serve tofu hot with toothpicks or forked picks.

MAKE AHEAD:
The sauce for Korma Tofu can be made up to 1 week ahead of serving if refrigerated, and up to 3 months ahead if frozen. Thaw and re-heat sauce before adding freshly baked tofu.

SAMOSAS

Makes 32 appetizer-sized pies

Samosas are little fried turnovers, made with all manner of fillings, but the most common is potatoes-and-peas. I've done a twist on the classic here, with protein-rich edamame standing in for carb-tastic peas.

--- Ingredients ---

Dough:

- 2 ½ cups all-purpose flour
- ½ cup semolina flour or cornmeal
- ¾ tsp. salt
- ¼ cup vegetable oil
- 1 cup hot water

Filling:

- two 15 oz. can potatoes (drained); or 3 fist-sized potatoes, cooked and peeled (bake, boil, or microwave); or 2 cups leftover mashed potatoes
- two 4 oz. cans diced mild green chile peppers
- 1 ½ cups frozen, shelled edamame (8 oz.), thawed
- 1 cup finely minced white or yellow onion (1 small onion)
- 1 Tbsp. finely minced or pressed garlic (3 large cloves)
- 1 Tbsp. grated fresh ginger root (peel and grate on a microplane or the super-fine side of a box grater) or 2 tsp. ground ginger
- 1 tsp. salt
- 1 tsp. garam masala (store bought or from recipe on page 89)
- ½ tsp. ground turmeric
- ½ tsp. ground cumin
- ½ tsp. ground coriander
- 1 tsp. lemon juice

Frying:

- 8 cups vegetable oil for deep frying (64 oz.)

Serving:

- 8 oz. jar tamarind or mango chutney (1 cup), or apricot chutney from recipe on page 94

Directions

1. **For dough:** In medium mixing bowl, combine all ingredients for dough.
2. Mix well with hands and knead until a smooth dough forms.
3. Set dough aside and let rest for 10 minutes. Prepare filling while dough rests.
4. **For filling:** In a medium mixing bowl, lightly mash potatoes with a potato masher or fork. Potatoes should be mashed but chunky.
5. Add remaining filling ingredients and stir until thoroughly mixed.
6. **For frying:** In a stockpot, deep frying pan, electric fryer, or wok, heat oil to 375° (a deep-fry thermometer is invaluable). Oil should be at least 3" deep. Line a baking sheet with several layers of paper towels or newspaper, lay a cooling rack upside down on top of paper, and set aside. While oil is heating, assemble samosas.
7. **To assemble:** Roll dough out into a thick snake and cut it into 16 equal portions. Using a rolling pin, flatten one portion of dough out into a 5" disk. Cut disk in half.
8. Place 1 tablespoon of filling on each semicircle of dough.
9. Fold the straight edge of one semicircle in half and pinch the straight edge together up and over the filling, creating a raised seam.
10. With the raised seam on the top of the samosa, tuck the filling in and pinch the open edge closed.
11. Repeat this process with the remaining dough and filling.
12. When the oil is up to temperature, drop samosas into oil. Do not crowd the pot—cook in batches as needed. Cook each batch for 5 minutes total, flipping samosas over as needed for even browning. Remove cooked samosas from oil using tongs or a kitchen spider. Lay on prepared tray to drain.
13. Allow oil to come back up to temperature before adding next batch of samosas.
14. Transfer fried samosas to a bowl or platter and serve warm with chutney on the side for dipping.

MAKE AHEAD:

Samosas can be made ahead and refrigerated for up to 4 days or frozen for up to 3 months. Thaw and lay out on a baking sheet. Re-heat in a 300° oven for 10 minutes.

GOING IT ALONE PARTY PREP COUNTDOWN

WEEKS BEFORE:
- ❏ Make and freeze Pizza Cinque Formaggi (Siciliana crust)
- ❏ Make and freeze Pizza Pugliese (Siciliana crust)
- ❏ Make and freeze Pizza Boscaiola (Romana crust)
- ❏ Make and freeze Pizza Vegetariana (Romana crust)
- ❏ Portion and freeze remaining half-batch of Romana crust
- ❏ Portion and freeze remaining Italian Pizza Sauce
- ❏ Make, portion, and freeze batch of Napoletana crust

4 DAYS BEFORE:
- ❏ Start veggies marinating for Marinated Veggie Skewers

2 DAYS BEFORE:
- ❏ Assemble marinated veggie skewers

1 DAY BEFORE:
- ❏ Make Lemon-Ricotta Cake
- ❏ Roast vegetables for Pizza di Patate (Potato)
- ❏ Prep toppings for Pizza ai Frutti di Mare (Seafood)

DAY OF PARTY:
Morning
- ❏ Remove all pre-made pizzas from freezer to thaw
- ❏ Remove Italian Pizza Sauce, Romana crusts, and Napoletana crusts from freezer to thaw
- ❏ Set up food table and choose all plates and platters for serving

2 Hours Before Party
- ❏ Organize crusts and toppings into "workstations" for: Pizza di Patate, Pizza ai Frutti di Mare, Pizza al Pesto Genovese, and Pizza Margherita

1½ Hour Before Party
- ❏ Preheat oven and pizza stone, if using

1 Hour Before Party
- ❏ Assemble and bake remaining pizzas in this order: Pizza di Patate, Pizza ai Fruitti di Mare, Pizza al Pesto Genovese, Pizza Margherita; bake pizzas together in oven, if possible
- ❏ Reduce oven temp and reheat together in oven: Pizza Cinque Formaggi + Pizza Pugliese on baking sheet on bottom rack; Pizza Boscaiola + Pizza Vegetariana on baking sheet on top rack

ITALY

PARTY FOR 12

This chapter had its genesis when I learned how decidedly different authentic Italian pizzas are from American pizzas. Different crust, different toppings, and no pepperoni. I know! No matter where you hail from, pizza-making is wildly creative and personal, but in Italy, preferences for style tend to be regional, centering on Naples, Rome, and Sicily. Each region boasts a distinctive crust—napoletana (thin, crispy, cracker-like crust typical of wood-fired oven pizzas), romana (a mid-weight crust), and siciliana (essentially a focaccia flatbread). This chapter features all three crusts and is organized around them —first the crust recipe, then the pizzas to be made on that crust. I have mapped out a way for one human person, on their own, to host this party and prepare—single-handedly!—all eight pizzas featured (for which you can thank me later).

Having said that, the least stressful way to throw this party is as a potluck. If I were hosting, I would make a batch of Italian Pizza Sauce and a batch of each of the crust doughs, portion and freeze all of them (instructions are given for this), and then distribute one recipe with one portion of sauce and one portion of the appropriate dough to each household attending. But you do you, and no matter how you manifest it, this chapter will yield an incredible, delicious, memorable, marvelous party!

VEGGIE SKEWERS

Makes 25 - 30 six-inch kebabs

These are a great do-ahead addition to any party. The veggies require a day or two to marinate, but demand virtually no time or attention. And the kebabs can be threaded a day or three before serving, which either takes one task off that last-minute list, or makes them perfect for carting to work with you, to be shared at an after-work gathering. Even better than all that, adding cubes of smoked or baked tofu to the mix makes these a vegan's dream-come-true. The oil in the marinade may thicken in the refrigerator, but once the kebabs come to room temperature, the oil will magically re-liquefy.

Ingredients

Marinade:

- ¼ cup red wine vinegar
- 2 Tbsp. extra virgin olive oil
- 1 Tbsp. balsamic vinegar
- 1 tsp. finely minced or pressed garlic (1 large clove)
- 1 tsp. dried basil
- ½ tsp. salt
- ¼ tsp. ground black pepper

Veggies:

- 8 oz. package fresh white mushrooms, cut in bite-sized pieces (cut top-to-bottom in halves or wedges)
- 8" zucchini squash, cut in ¼" thick half-moons
- 1 red or yellow bell pepper, seeded and cut in 1" pieces
- 1 pint cherry tomatoes (2 cups)
- ½ red onion, cut in 1" pieces or 15 oz. jar whole pearl onions, drained

Skewers:

- 25–30 six-inch bamboo skewers

Directions

1. In a large, non-reactive mixing bowl (no aluminum), combine all ingredients for the marinade. Mix with a whisk or fork to blend.
2. Add the veggies to the marinade in the bowl. Stir gently to coat veggies.
3. Cover and refrigerate veggie mix for at least 24 hours (48 hours is even better), gently stirring the mixture once or twice a day, to be sure that all the veggies get marinated.
4. Once the veggie mix is fully marinated, thread veggies in a random order onto skewers, making each kebab different.
5. Lay kebabs on a platter and serve at room temperature.

MAKE AHEAD:
Veggies can be marinated up to 5 days ahead and skewers can be threaded up to three days ahead of serving. Keep covered and refrigerated.

LEMON-RICOTTA CAKE
Makes 9" round cake

This lovely cake is moist, lemony, and positively yummy. It is also dense enough to be terribly well-behaved when picked up and eaten without utensils. And if that isn't enough to win you over, it requires no frosting, ever!

Ingredients

Cake:

- 1 ½ cups granulated sugar
- 1 ½ cups whole milk ricotta cheese (15 oz. carton)
- ½ cup vegetable oil
- zest and juice of 2 large lemons (4 tsp. zest + ½ cup juice, strained of seeds)
- 4 large eggs
- 1 tsp. lemon extract
- 1 tsp. vanilla extract
- 1 ½ cups all-purpose flour
- ½ cup cornstarch
- 1 ½ tsp. baking powder
- 1 tsp. baking soda
- ½ tsp. salt

Topping:

- 2 tsp. confectioner's sugar

MAKE AHEAD:
Lemon-Ricotta Cake can be made the day before serving. Keep tightly covered at room temperature.

Directions

1. Generously grease and flour a 9" springform pan or tube pan (as for bundt cake or angel food cake). Set aside.
2. Preheat oven to 350°.
3. **For cake:** In a large mixing bowl, combine sugar, ricotta, oil, zest, juice, eggs, and extracts. Beat with a whisk until emulsified.
4. Add remaining ingredients. Mix with whisk until blended and smooth. Do not over-mix or cake will be tough.
5. Transfer batter to prepared pan. Spread to an even layer.
6. Bake cake for 50–60 minutes, until top of cake springs back when touched and a pick inserted in the center of cake comes out clean.
7. Allow cake to cool in pan for 15 minutes. Remove cake from pan and allow to cool completely on a cooling rack.
8. Transfer cake to a serving plate. Dust top of cake with confectioner's sugar by shaking sugar through a strainer. To serve, cut cake in 16 wedges with a serrated bread knife. Cake can be kept at room temperature for 2 days, then must be refrigerated.

NAPOLETANA PIZZA CRUST

Makes two 12" thin pizza crusts

This crust is distinctively thin, crispy, and a standard for pizzas cooked in a wood-fired oven. If you don't have a fancy wood-fired pizza oven, you can achieve that perfect crust with a hot pizza stone as well. If you don't have one of those, either, do not fret. This crust is spectacular baked on a regular pan in a regular oven.

Ingredients

- 1 ⅔ cups all-purpose flour
- 1 packet active dry yeast (2 ¼ tsp.)
- ⅔ cup lukewarm water
- ½ tsp. salt

Directions

1. In a medium mixing bowl, combine flour and yeast.
2. Add water. With a wooden spoon, mix until water is thoroughly incorporated. Dough will be lumpy and a bit crumbly.
3. Let dough rest for 10 minutes. Turn dough out onto a clean work surface. Add the salt. Using hands, knead the dough until the salt is incorporated and the dough is smooth and elastic (about 5 minutes). Dough should remain slightly sticky.
4. Grease the mixing bowl with oil or spray oil, and return dough to bowl. Turn and flip dough so all sides of dough are covered with oil.
5. Cover bowl with a damp towel. Set bowl in a warm place for dough to rise until tripled in volume (about 3 hours).
6. Punch dough down, divide in half, and knead each portion for a minute or so. Coat each portion with a spray or drizzle of olive oil and return them to the bowl. Cover bowl and allow to rise another hour.
7. Gently press and stretch each portion out to a 12" disc.
8. Proceed with your chosen pizza recipe(s).

MAKE AHEAD:
Napoletana Pizza Crust can be made well ahead of baking and serving. Prepare the dough through step #5, punch down, divide in half, place each portion in a quart-sized ziptop freezer bag, and freeze for up to 3 months. To make a pizza, remove one portion of dough from the freezer and allow to thaw at room temperature for 6–8 hours (in its bag). Press dough into a 12" disc and proceed with recipe.

PIZZA AL PESTO GENOVESE
Makes 12" thin-crust pizza

Similar to a Margherita pizza, with the same thin, crispy crust, this pizza hails from a different region of Italy and has no tomatoes on it. Simple, and simply divine!

Ingredients

Crust:

- one 12" Napoletana Pizza Crust from recipe on page 107

Toppings:

- ⅓ cup pesto sauce (3 oz.)
- 8 oz. buffalo mozzarella or fresh mozzarella

Directions

1. Preheat oven to 500°. If using a pizza stone, place stone on bottom rack of oven. Oven and stone need to be at temperature for 30 minutes before pizza goes in.
2. **To assemble:** Pat and stretch dough out to a cracker-thin 12" disc. If the dough resists stretching, let it rest for 5–10 minutes and try again.
3. If using a pizza stone for baking, sprinkle 2 tablespoons semolina flour on a pizza peel and lay circle of dough on it. Otherwise, grease a pizza pan or baking sheet, and lay the disc of dough on it. Stretch dough back into a 12" round disc.
4. Spread sauce evenly over crust, keeping it ½" in from the edge.
5. Tear mozzarella into small chunks. Scatter pieces over sauce.
6. If using a pizza stone, shake pizza off peel and onto stone. Bake for 8–10 minutes, until crust is brown around edges. If baking pizza on a pan, bake on middle rack of oven for 10–12 minutes, until bottom is crispy and edges are browned.
7. Remove pizza, allow to cool slightly, then cut in 16 wedges and serve. This pizza should be served freshly made and not re-heated.

VEGETARIAN

PIZZA MARGHERITA

Makes 12" thin-crust pizza

The gold standard Margherita pizza is made with garden fresh tomato slices and has to be eaten as soon as it comes out of the oven. Any delay in consumption allows the crust to absorb tomato juices and become soggy. Since this particular Margherita pizza needs to stand up to hours on a party buffet, I have eschewed fresh tomatoes and enlisted flavorful, sun-dried tomatoes in their place.

Ingredients

Crust:

- one 12" Napoletana Pizza Crust from recipe on page 107

Toppings:

- 1 Tbsp. olive oil
- 8 oz. fresh mozzarella, thinly sliced
- ½ cup sun-dried tomatoes, julienne-cut (4 oz.; drain if in oil)
- 3 Tbsp. fresh basil leaves
- 1 tsp. finely minced or pressed garlic (1 large clove)

Directions

1. Preheat oven to 500°. If using a pizza stone, place stone on bottom rack of oven. Oven and stone need to be at temperature for 30 minutes before pizza goes in.
2. **To assemble:** Pat and stretch dough out to a cracker-thin 12" disc. If the dough resists stretching, let it rest for 5–10 minutes and try again.
3. If using a pizza stone for baking, sprinkle 2 tablespoons semolina flour on a pizza peel and lay the disc of dough on it. Otherwise, grease a pizza pan or baking sheet, and lay the disc of dough on it. Stretch dough back into a 12" round disc.
4. Spread olive oil evenly over crust, extending all the way to the edges (use fingers or a pastry brush).
5. Lay mozzarella slices over crust.
6. Scatter tomatoes over cheese.
7. Cut basil in a chiffonade (stack basil leaves, roll up lengthwise, then cut crosswise in narrow strips). Scatter basil and then garlic on pizza.
8. If using a pizza stone, shake pizza off peel and onto stone. Bake for 8–10 minutes, until crust is brown around edges. If baking pizza on a pan, bake on middle rack of oven for 10–12 minutes, until bottom is crispy and edges are browned.
9. Remove pizza, allow to cool slightly, then cut in 16 wedges and serve. This pizza should be served freshly made and not re-heated.

VEGETARIAN

ROMANA PIZZA CRUST

Makes four 12" pizza crusts

This crust is what most Americans would call "hand-tossed." But it is oh-so-much more than that. Boasting flavor and texture reminiscent of sourdough, this crust will test your patience AND reward your taste buds. A sourdough sponge is the secret of all. Give the sponge a one to two day head start and it will yield the most extraordinary pizza crust you've ever had. Well worth the wait!

Ingredients

Sourdough Sponge:

- 1 ½ cups water warmed to 105°–115° (should feel like warm bath water)
- ¼ tsp. active dry yeast (part of one packet—save rest for dough)
- 3 cups all-purpose flour

Dough:

- 1 ½ cups lukewarm water
- rest of the packet of active dry yeast (2 tsp.)
- 3 ¾ cups bread flour
- ½ cup olive oil
- 1 Tbsp. salt

MAKE AHEAD:
Romana Pizza Crust can be made well ahead of baking and serving. Prepare the dough through step #10, place each portion in a quart-sized ziptop freezer bag, and freeze for up to 3 months. To make a pizza, remove one portion of dough from the freezer and allow to thaw at room temperature for 6–8 hours (in its bag). Press dough into a 12" disc and proceed with recipe.

Directions

1. **For sourdough sponge:** In a large mixing bowl, dissolve yeast in warm water and let sit for 5 minutes.
2. Add flour and stir until no lumps of flour remain.
3. Cover bowl with a damp towel and let sit at room temperature for 24 to 48 hours.
4. **For dough:** After the sourdough sponge is ready, use it as a base for the dough.
5. Add the water and yeast to the sourdough. Stir. Let mixture sit for 5 minutes for yeast to dissolve and activate.
6. Add remaining ingredients for dough. Stir until dough is smooth and sticky.
7. Cover bowl with a damp towel and let dough rise at room temperature for 1 hour.
8. Using greased hands or two forks, lift and fold the dough over itself. Grab it from underneath and fold north-over-south, then east-over-west. Turn the bowl ¼ turn and do those folds again.
9. Re-cover bowl and set aside for 1 hour. Repeat the folding process, cover, and set aside for 1 hour more (2 foldings and 3 risings in all).
10. Deflate dough and turn out onto a well-floured work surface. Divide dough into four equal pieces. Shape each into a ball, coating the outside with a dusting of flour.
11. Gently press and stretch each portion out to a 12" disc. Proceed with your chosen pizza recipe(s).
12. **NOTE:** If something happens to prevent you from using this dough to make pizzas on the day described, prepare the dough through step #9 and fold again. Cover the bowl with plastic wrap and refrigerate for up to 3 days, folding the dough once each day. Remove the dough from the refrigerator several hours before shaping into crusts, to allow it to come to room temperature.

VEGAN

PIZZA AI FRUTTI DI MARE (SEAFOOD)

Makes 12" pizza

Italy is a country of endless seashores, so of course Italians enjoy a bountiful seafood pizza. As a bonus, this incredible pizza has no cheese on it, so is dairy-free.

Ingredients

Crust:

- one 12" Romana Crust from recipe on opposite page

Toppings:

- ½ cup Italian pizza sauce from recipe on page 115
- 6.5 oz. can chopped clams, drained (save nectar and freeze for a later fish soup)
- 8 oz. package raw calamari (squid), cleaned, bodies cut in ½" slices, tentacles left in clusters
- 8 oz. package raw shrimp, peeled, de-veined, and cut in half lengthwise (if frozen, thaw)
- ½ cup sliced green onions (2–3 onions)
- 1 large clove garlic, finely minced or pressed (1 tsp.)
- drizzle of olive oil

MAKE AHEAD:

Pizza ai Frutti di Mare can be made up to 2 days ahead of serving. Bake pizza, allow to cool completely, wrap tightly, and refrigerate. Re-heat pizza on a baking sheet in a 300° oven for 10 minutes. Cut in wedges after re-heating.

Directions

1. Preheat oven to 500°. If using a pizza stone, place stone on middle rack of oven. Oven and stone need to be at temperature for 30 minutes before pizza goes in.

2. **To assemble:** If using a pizza stone for baking, sprinkle 2 tablespoons semolina flour on a pizza peel and lay disc of crust dough on it. If using a pizza pan or baking sheet, grease pan and lay dough on top. Stretch dough back into a 12" round disc. Let dough rest and rise for 30 minutes.

3. Spread sauce on crust using the back of a spoon. Distribute evenly, staying ½" in from the edge.

4. Top crust with remaining toppings, in the order listed. Sprinkle each evenly across the surface of the crust, then drizzle lightly with olive oil. If including calamari tentacle clusters, lay them out open, like a flower, so they cook evenly.

5. If using a pizza stone, slide pizza off peel and onto stone. Bake until the crust is golden brown and shrimp are pink and opaque, about 12–15 minutes. Otherwise, place pizza on its baking sheet on the middle rack in the oven and bake for 15–20 minutes. Crust should be browned on the bottom and shrimp should be pink and opaque.

6. Remove pizza from oven, allow to cool slightly, then cut in 16 wedges and serve.

PIZZA DI PATATE (POTATO)
Makes one 12" pizza

I agree with you, raw fennel on a pizza sounds super-yucky. But roasted fennel? Super-yummy! With roasting, the licorice flavor cooks out and a sweet, caramelized flavor replaces it. It is the perfect companion for potatoes and onions. And yes, the combination is very Italian and very phenomenal on pizza.

--- Ingredients ---

Crust:

- one 12" Romana Crust from recipe on page 110

Roasted Vegetables:

- 1 fennel bulb
- 1 medium white or yellow onion
- 2 fist-sized potatoes (1 lb.)
- 2 Tbsp. olive oil
- ½ tsp. salt

Toppings:

- ½ cup Italian pizza sauce from recipe on page 115
- 2 tsp. fresh rosemary leaves or 1 tsp. dried rosemary
- 1 tsp. fresh thyme leaves or ½ tsp. dried thyme
- ¼ tsp. ground black pepper
- 8 oz. package shredded 6-Cheese Italian Blend (2 cups) or sliced Provolone cheese

Directions

1. **For roasted vegetables:** Preheat oven to 400°.
2. Cut top and root ends off fennel bulb. Remove any damaged outer bits. Cut bulb in half top-to-bottom and then in very thin wedges. Peel the onion and cut it the same way.
3. Scrub potatoes but do not peel. Cut in thin, ⅛" slices.
4. In a 9" x 13" baking pan, combine fennel, onions, and potatoes. Drizzle with oil and salt. Mix everything together until coated in oil.
5. Roast vegetables for 60 minutes. Stir every 15 minutes.
6. Remove roasted vegetables from oven and transfer to a bowl to cool. Vegetables may be roasted up to 3 days ahead of assembly of pizza. Keep them covered and refrigerated.
7. Turn oven up to 500°. If using a pizza stone, place stone on bottom rack of oven.
8. **To assemble:** If using a pizza stone for baking, sprinkle 2 tablespoons semolina flour on a pizza peel and lay disc of crust dough on it. If using a pizza pan or baking sheet, grease pan and lay dough on top. Stretch dough back out to a 12" diameter. Let dough rest and rise for 30 minutes.
9. Spread sauce on crust using the back of a spoon. Distribute evenly, staying ½" in from the edge.
10. Top this with the roasted vegetables, distributing them evenly. Sprinkle rosemary, thyme, and pepper over vegetables.
11. Top everything with cheese.
12. If using a pizza stone, slide pizza off peel and onto stone. Bake until the crust is browned, about 12–15 minutes. Otherwise, place pizza on its baking sheet on the middle rack of the oven. Bake for 15–20 minutes, until crust is browned and cheese is beginning to brown on top.
13. Remove pizza from oven, allow to cool slightly, then cut in 16 wedges and serve.

> **MAKE AHEAD:**
> Pizza di Patate can be made up to 2 days ahead of serving. Bake pizza, allow to cool completely, wrap tightly, and refrigerate. Re-heat pizza on a baking sheet in a 300° oven for 10 minutes. Cut in wedges after re-heating.

PIZZA VEGETARIANA

Makes one 12" pizza

Italian veggie pizza is quite different from its American counterpart. Unlike American pizza that is topped with fresh vegetables that barely cook, Pizza Vegetariana employs pre-roasting to bring a depth of flavor to the eggplant, plus a combination of fresh and cooked toppings that create a balance of tantalizing flavors.

Ingredients

Crust:
- one 12" Romana Crust from recipe on page 110

Eggplant:
- 1 Tbsp. olive oil
- 1 baby eggplant, cut in ½" slices

Toppings:
- ½ cup Italian pizza sauce from recipe on opposite page
- ½ cup ricotta cheese
- 14 oz. can artichoke hearts, drained and cut in thin wedges
- 3 large cloves garlic, finely minced or pressed (1 Tbsp.)
- 1 to 2 Tbsp. peperoncini peppers, drained and minced
- 1 Tbsp. minced fresh basil or 1 tsp. dried basil
- 8 oz. package sliced Provolone cheese

Directions

1. If using a pizza stone, place stone on bottom rack of oven.
2. **For eggplant:** Preheat oven to 400°. Brush olive oil on each side of the eggplant slices. Lay slices out on a baking sheet.
3. Roast eggplant for 45 minutes (on center rack of oven), flipping slices over in the middle of roasting. While eggplant roasts, prepare crust.
4. **To assemble:** If using a pizza stone for baking, sprinkle 2 tablespoons semolina flour on a pizza peel and lay disc of crust dough on it. If using a pizza pan or baking sheet, grease pan and lay dough on top. Stretch dough back out to a 12" diameter. Let dough rest and rise for 30 minutes.
5. Turn oven up to 500°.
6. Spread sauce on crust using the back of a spoon. Distribute evenly, staying ½" in from the edge.
7. Top this with small dollops of ricotta.
8. Lay the eggplant slices on top, distributing evenly. Top these with artichokes, garlic, peppers, basil, and then Provolone cheese.
9. If using a pizza stone, slide pizza off peel and onto stone. Bake until the crust is browned, about 12–15 minutes. Otherwise, place pizza on its baking sheet on the middle rack of the oven. Bake for 15–20 minutes, until crust is browned and cheese is beginning to brown on top.
10. Remove pizza from oven, allow to cool slightly, then cut in 16 wedges and serve.

MAKE AHEAD:
Pizza Vegetariana can be made ahead of serving. Bake pizza, allow to cool completely, wrap tightly, and refrigerate up to 2 days or freeze for up to 1 month. Thaw and re-heat pizza on a baking sheet in a 300° oven for 10 minutes. Cut in wedges after re-heating.

Pizza Vegetariana

ITALIAN PIZZA SAUCE
Makes 3 ½ cups

American pizza sauce is heavily seasoned and herbed, but Italian sauce is not. Basically just tomatoes, this Italian sauce is the perfect base for all the flavors that sit atop an Italian pizza.

Ingredients
- 28 oz. can crushed tomatoes
- 6 oz. can tomato paste
- 1 Tbsp. finely minced or pressed garlic (3 large cloves)
- 1 tsp. salt

Directions
1. In a medium mixing bowl, combine all ingredients. Stir with a whisk to fully incorporate tomato paste.
2. Transfer sauce to a covered container and refrigerate.

MAKE AHEAD:
Italian Pizza Sauce can be made up to 1 week ahead of use if refrigerated, and up to 12 months ahead if frozen. Keep in a tightly covered container, or freeze in an ice cube tray, then transfer frozen cubes to a ziptop bag.

VEGAN

PIZZA BOSCAIOLA (SAUSAGE AND PEPPERS)

Makes 12" pizza

A perfect pairing of creamy Alfredo sauce, herby sausage, and roasted sweet peppers. Just fantastic!

Ingredients

Crust:

- one 12" Romana Pizza Crust from recipe on page 110

Alfredo Sauce:

- 2 Tbsp. butter (do not substitute margarine)
- ½ cup heavy cream
- ½ cup shredded Parmesan cheese
- 1 Tbsp. minced fresh parsley or 1 tsp. dried parsley

Toppings:

- ½ cup shredded Pecorino Romano cheese (or Parmesan cheese; 2–3 oz.)
- 8 oz. shredded mozzarella cheese (2 cups)
- 6 oz. thinly sliced meatless veggie Italian sausage (½ of a 12 oz. package)
- 8 oz. jar roasted red bell pepper strips, drained (or 1 roasted, peeled, sliced red pepper)

> **MAKE AHEAD:**
> Pizza Boscaiola can be made ahead of serving. Bake pizza, allow to cool completely, wrap tightly, and refrigerate up to 2 days or freeze for up to 1 month. Thaw and re-heat pizza on a baking sheet in a 300° oven for 10 minutes. Cut in wedges after re-heating.

Directions

1. Preheat oven to 500°. If using a pizza stone, place stone on bottom rack of oven.
2. **To assemble:** If using a pizza stone for baking, sprinkle 2 tablespoons semolina flour on a pizza peel and lay disc of crust dough on it. If using a pizza pan or baking sheet, grease pan and lay dough on top. Stretch dough back out to a 12" diameter. Let dough rest and rise for 30 minutes. While dough rests, make Alfredo sauce.
3. **For Alfredo sauce:** In a small sauce pan over medium heat, melt butter.
4. Add cream, stir, and heat to a simmer (bubbles will form around edge of pan, but mixture should not boil). Add cheese and parsley. Stir in. Bring back to a simmer. Cook and stir for 1 minute. Remove pan from heat.
5. When crust has risen, gently spread Alfredo sauce on dough using the back of a spoon. Distribute evenly, staying ½" in from the outer edge.
6. Completely cover sauce with Pecorino Romano cheese. Top this with mozzarella.
7. Scatter sausage and peppers over top of pizza.
8. If using a pizza stone, slide pizza off peel and onto stone. Bake until the crust is browned, about 12–15 minutes. Otherwise, place pizza on its baking sheet on the middle rack of the oven. Bake for 15–20 minutes, until crust is browned and cheese is beginning to brown on top.
9. Remove pizza from oven, allow to cool slightly, then cut in 16 wedges and serve.

SICILIANA PIZZA CRUST

Makes two 9" x 13" pan pizzas

Siciliana Pizza Crust is the loftiest, breadiest of crusts, much like a focaccia or ciabatta. It makes a lovely, sturdy base for lots of sauce and cheese, but the Italian way of making it creates an open texture that keeps it light and digestible (not like a lump in your gut). Making it begins with the creation of scalded flour, so plan ahead—this crust must be started the day before you intend to use it. And please don't skip the scald—it enables the flour to absorb more moisture for crust tenderness.

Ingredients

Scald:
- ½ cup bread flour
- 1 ½ cups boiling water

Dough:
- 1 packet active dry yeast (2 ¼ tsp.)
- 2 ½ cups bread flour
- 1 tsp. salt
- 2 Tbsp. olive oil

Pans:
- 6 Tbsp. olive oil

MAKE AHEAD:
Siciliana Pizza Crust can be made well ahead of baking and serving. Prepare the dough through step #7, divide in half, place each portion in a quart-sized ziptop freezer bag, and freeze up to 3 months ahead of baking. To make a pizza, remove one portion of dough from the freezer and allow to thaw at room temperature for 6–8 hours (in its bag).

Directions

1. **For scald:** In a large mixing bowl, combine flour and boiling water. Stir like crazy for 1 minute, until mixture is gluey.
2. Cover bowl with a damp towel. Allow mixture to sit at room temperature for 12–24 hours for flour to fully hydrate.
3. **For dough:** Add yeast to finished scald. Stir and let sit for 5 minutes for yeast to dissolve.
4. Add remaining ingredients for dough. Stir until a sticky, lumpy dough forms.
5. Cover bowl with a damp towel. Let sit at room temperature for 30 minutes.
6. Using greased hands or two forks, lift and fold the dough over itself. Grab it from underneath and fold north-over-south, then east-over-west. Turn the bowl ¼ turn and repeat those folds.
7. Re-cover bowl and set aside for 30 minutes. Repeat the folding process every 30 minutes, for a total of 7 times (3 hours total from when you finished mixing the dough).
8. After final 30 minute rise, drizzle 2 tablespoons olive oil in each of two 9" x 13" pans.
9. Divide dough in half. Transfer each portion of dough to a prepared baking pan. Top each dough with 1 tablespoon oil. Press the dough into the pans, forming flat crusts that fill the pans edge-to-edge and do not have a raised rim. This will take 30 minutes, as the dough will be elastic and will resist stretching. Stretch as much as you can, let dough rest 15 minutes, stretch again, rest again, and stretch a final time. Do this gently so you don't completely deflate the dough.
10. Allow crusts to rise 30 minutes, then proceed with your chosen recipe.

VEGAN

PIZZA CINQUE FORMAGGI (5-CHEESE)

Makes 9" x 13" thick-crust pizza

Plain cheese pizza sounds boring, so this one will come as a surprise. A mix of soft cheeses, spinach, and garlic hides under the "plain old" cheese topping, giving this pizza a nice kick of flavors.

Ingredients

Crust:

- one 9" x 13" Siciliana Crust from recipe on page 117

Toppings:

- 8 oz. package chevre goat cheese
- ½ cup ricotta cheese (5 oz.)
- 5 oz. package fresh spinach, coarsely chopped
- 3 large cloves garlic, minced (1 Tbsp.) and smashed into a paste with ¼ tsp. salt
- ½ cup Italian pizza sauce from recipe on page 115
- 2 oz. grated asiago cheese (1 cup)
- 4 oz. shredded fontina cheese (1 cup)
- 8 oz. shredded mozzarella cheese (2 cups)
- 1 Tbsp. minced fresh basil or ½ tsp. dried basil
- 1 tsp. finely minced or pressed garlic (1 large clove)

MAKE AHEAD:
Pizza Cinque Formaggi can be made ahead of serving. Bake pizza, allow to cool completely, wrap tightly, and refrigerate up to 2 days or freeze for up to 1 month. Thaw and re-heat pizza on a baking sheet in a 300° oven for 10 minutes. Slice pizza after re-heating.

VEGETARIAN

Directions

1. Preheat oven to 450°.
2. In a medium mixing bowl, combine goat cheese, ricotta, spinach, and garlic with salt. Stir and toss to mix well. Set aside.
3. Spoon pizza sauce onto risen crust. With the back of the spoon, gently spread sauce over surface, creating an even layer all the way to the edges.
4. Bake crust on lowest rack of oven for 10 minutes. While crust bakes, get all toppings at the ready.
5. Remove crust from oven and work as quickly as possible to top it. Spoon spinach-cheese mixture in small dollops onto crust.
6. Sprinkle cheeses evenly over pizza. Top with basil and garlic.
7. Return pizza to oven, onto the middle rack. Bake an additional 20–30 minutes, until cheese is golden brown on top.
8. Remove pizza from pan, and place on a cutting board. Allow to cool slightly, then cut into 16 squares using a serrated knife. Transfer pizza to a serving platter and serve hot.

PIZZA PUGLIESE

Makes 9" x 13" thick-crust pizza

Those Italians know how to top a pizza! Each of the toppings here packs a punch on its own, but together they create a beautiful symphony of flavor.

—— Ingredients ——

Crust:

- one 9" x 13" Siciliana Crust from recipe on page 117

Toppings:

- ½ cup Italian pizza sauce from recipe on page 115
- 8 oz. shredded mozzarella cheese (2 cups)
- 8 oz. sliced or shredded Provolone cheese (2 cups)
- ½ cup sliced kalamata or black olives (2 oz.)
- 1 cup cherry tomatoes, cut in half (half pint) or ½ cup sun-dried tomatoes
- 1 medium red onion, sliced in thin rings (2 cups)

MAKE AHEAD:
Pizza Pugliese can be made ahead of serving. Bake pizza, allow to cool completely, wrap tightly, and refrigerate up to 2 days or freeze for up to 1 month. Thaw and re-heat pizza on a baking sheet in a 300° oven for 10 minutes. Slice pizza after re-heating.

—— Directions ——

1. Preheat oven to 450°.
2. Spoon pizza sauce onto risen crust. With the back of the spoon, gently spread sauce over surface, creating an even layer all the way to the edges.
3. Bake crust on lowest rack of oven for 10 minutes. While crust is in the oven, get toppings at the ready.
4. Remove crust from oven and work as quickly as possible to top it.
5. Sprinkle cheeses evenly over pizza. Top with olives, tomatoes, and onions, in that order. The pizza will appear to have an overkill of onions. Trust this recipe and don't take any onions off.
6. Return pizza to oven, onto the middle rack. Bake an additional 20–30 minutes, until cheese is golden brown on top.
7. Remove pizza from pan, and place on a cutting board. Allow to cool slightly, then cut into 16 squares using a serrated knife. Transfer pizza to a serving platter and serve hot.

GOING IT ALONE PARTY PREP COUNTDOWN

WEEKS BEFORE:
- ❏ Make Cilantro Pesto for Quesadillas and freeze
- ❏ Make Chipotle Fish Fritters and freeze
- ❏ Make Empanadas and freeze

3 DAYS BEFORE:
- ❏ Make Molé Brownies
- ❏ Make Chipotle Aioli
- ❏ Make Salsa Verde
- ❏ Make seasoning mix for Watermelon Kebabs

2 DAYS BEFORE:
- ❏ Make Rajas Con Queso Dip (do not bake)
- ❏ Make Stuffed Jalapeños (do not bake)

1 DAY BEFORE:
- ❏ Make Shrimp Salsa
- ❏ Make slaw for Fish Tacos
- ❏ Remove from freezer to thaw: Cilantro Pesto, Chipotle Fish Fritters, Empanadas

DAY OF PARTY:
Morning
- ❏ Set up food table and choose platters, bowls, and trays for serving all dishes
- ❏ Make Avocado Dip
- ❏ Cut Watermelon and thread on skewers

90 Minutes Before Party
- ❏ Make Quesadillas
- ❏ Make Fish Tacos
- ❏ Bake: Rajas Con Queso Dip, Stuffed Jalapeños
- ❏ Re-heat: Chipotle Fish Fritters, Empanadas
- ❏ Season Watermelon Kebabs

MEXICO

PARTY FOR 24

I've only been to Mexico once, but my lasting impression is of Color! Color! Color! The landscape bursting with flowers, the trees displaying every green in the big crayon box, the people dressed in vivid layers of color, and the incredible food displayed on exuberant handmade pottery. This chapter, this party, seeks to capture the colors and flavors of Mexico with the fresh ingredients in one dish complementing the slow-simmered sauce of another, and the heat of native spices setting off the sweet notes in peppers, seafood, and fruit. This menu encompasses bold heat from the Stuffed Jalapeños to the Chipotle Fish Fritters, balanced out by the mildness of things like the Avocado Dip and Molé Brownies. If you are flying solo and making this entire chapter on your own, planning is key, as you will need to do some cooking and prep every day after work, in the days leading up to your party. It is very do-able, not overwhelming at all, and the sensational results will be totally worth your efforts!*

SPICED WATERMELON SKEWERS

Makes 48 skewers

This is a popular snack in Mexico, and for good reason. The refreshing juiciness of the watermelon combines with the salty heat of the spice blend for a phenomenal taste sensation. You can cut the watermelon ahead of time (keep it covered and chilled), but don't season it until the last minute. The salt in the seasoning mix is essential, but it will draw moisture out of the watermelon.

Ingredients

Spice Blend:

- 2 Tbsp. lime juice powder or 1 Tbsp. fresh lime zest (2 limes)
- 1 Tbsp. chili powder
- 2 tsp. smoked paprika
- 1 tsp. granulated sugar
- 1 tsp. salt
- ½ tsp. ground chipotle pepper

Melon:

- 1 small, round watermelon, cut in 1" cubes (rind removed; about 12 cups)
- 48 six-inch bamboo skewers, or equivalent 4.5" picks

Directions

1. In a salt shaker or mug, mix ingredients for spice blend.
2. Thread cubes of melon onto skewers.
3. Lay skewers out on a work surface. Press them close together, in a single layer.
4. Shake or sprinkle spice blend over watermelon. Flip skewers over and sprinkle more spice on.
5. Transfer skewers to a serving platter and serve at once.

MAKE AHEAD:
The spice blend can be made up to 1 week ahead of serving (refrigerate if using fresh zest). The watermelon can be cut and skewered up to 2 days ahead of serving, but do not season the skewers until just before serving.

VEGAN

SALSA VERDE

Makes 1 ½ cups

Fresh, hot, sweet, creamy, and good-looking to boot—this salsa is sensational! If you are a gardener (or know one … .), you can make this with green, unripe tomatoes in place of the tomatillos. Outstanding as a counterpoint and alternative to red salsa.

Ingredients

- 1 large, ripe avocado (1 cup flesh)
- ¾ cup diced tomatillos (4–6 fruits; let ripen at room temperature until papery covering is dry, remove covering and wash sticky substance off fruits)
- 4 oz. can mild, diced green chile peppers
- ¼ cup finely minced white or yellow onion
- ½ jalapeño pepper, finely minced (leave seeds in for hot salsa; remove seeds for milder)
- 2 Tbsp. finely minced fresh cilantro leaves
- 1 tsp. minced garlic (1 large clove), smashed to a paste with ¼ tsp. salt
- 1 Tbsp. vegetable oil
- 1 Tbsp. lime juice (½ of a lime)
- 1 tsp. agave or granulated sugar

Serving:

- 8 oz. bag tortilla chips

Directions

1. Cut avocado in half top-to-bottom, remove pit, and scoop flesh into a small mixing bowl. Remove any bruises or brown spots as you go. Mash avocado flesh with a fork.
2. Add remaining ingredients to bowl. Stir until well mixed.
3. Taste, and adjust seasonings.
4. Transfer salsa to a covered container and refrigerate until needed. Serve salsa chilled with tortilla chips for scooping.

MAKE AHEAD:
Salsa Verde can be made up to 3 days before serving. Keep covered and refrigerated.

VEGAN

SHRIMP SALSA

Makes 4 cups

I am pretty sure that this salsa was my own crazy idea, combining traditional salsa ingredients with non-traditional elements like shrimp, cucumber, and celery. Fresh, beautiful, delicious, and unforgettable, I love this dish. And I love taking it to potluck parties where it is always received as an unexpected, most welcome addition.

Ingredients

Salsa:

- 1 lb. cooked, peeled, deveined shrimp
- 14 oz. can fire roasted, diced tomatoes, drained (drink juice or save for another use)
- 1 cup finely diced cucumber, peeled, with large seeds removed (6" cucumber)
- 1 cup finely diced celery (2 large ribs)
- 1/4 cup sliced green onions (1 - 2 onions)
- 1 clove garlic, minced (1 tsp.) and smashed to a paste with 1/2 tsp. salt
- 1 jalapeño pepper, seeded and very finely minced (leave seeds in for a hot salsa)
- 1 Tbsp. finely minced fresh cilantro
- 2 Tbsp. olive oil
- 1 Tbsp. fresh lime juice (1/2 of a lime)

Serving:

- 8 oz. bag tortilla chips

Directions

1. Cut shrimp into ¼" pieces and place in a medium mixing bowl.
2. Add remaining salsa ingredients and gently stir the shrimp and vegetables together.
3. Taste and adjust seasonings. Refrigerate until serving time. Serve Shrimp Salsa chilled with tortilla chips on the side for scooping.

MAKE AHEAD:
Shrimp Salsa can be made 1 day ahead of serving. Keep covered and refrigerated.

SEAFOOD

AVOCADO DIP

Makes 4 cups

Guacamole is a finicky thing, and must be made moments before serving, because any delay will give it a chance to turn an unappetizing shade of brown. This dip, on the other hand, can be made up to 24 hours before serving, with no browning. The addition of cream cheese and artichokes makes all the difference, and the finished dip has a wonderful texture and flavor profile. Great on just about anything, or on its own scooped onto tortilla chips.

Ingredients

Dip:

- 8 oz. package cream cheese, at room temperature
- 2 large or 3 small avocados (3 cups flesh)
- 1 Tbsp. lime juice (½ lime)
- 14 oz. can artichoke hearts, drained and chopped very fine
- ¾ cup sliced or chopped black olives (4 oz.)
- 1 large clove garlic (1 tsp.), minced and smashed into a paste with ¼ tsp. salt
- 1 green onion, thinly sliced (3 Tbsp.)
- ½ tsp. dried dill weed
- ½ tsp. ground cumin

Serving:

- 8 oz. bag tortilla chips

Directions

1. **For Dip:** In a medium mixing bowl, soften cream cheese by mashing it with a sturdy spatula or the back of a wooden spoon.
2. Cut avocados in half. Remove pits and scoop flesh into mixing bowl. Remove and discard any bruised flesh or brown spots as you go.
3. Add lime juice to bowl.
4. Mash avocados with a fork and blend into cream cheese.
5. Add remaining ingredients and stir vigorously to blend in.
6. Cover and refrigerate until serving time.
7. Serve dip as a condiment for any Mexican dish, or with tortilla chips on the side for scooping.

MAKE AHEAD:
Avocado Dip can be made the day before serving. Keep tightly covered and refrigerated.

STUFFED JALAPEÑOS

Makes 24–32 appetizers

These are so quick and delicious! No Mexican buffet would be complete without stuffed peppers, and these combine the best of hot, creamy, and smoky.

Ingredients

Peppers:

- 12 large or 16 small jalapeño peppers (more if you plan to leave the seeds in for super-hot stuffed peppers)

Filling:

- 4 oz. cream cheese, at room temperature (½ of an 8 oz. block)
- 6 oz. grated smoked mozzarella or smoked cheddar cheese (1 ½ cups)
- 5 oz. package smoky tempeh or other vegetarian bacon, diced
- 3 large cloves garlic, minced (1 Tbsp.) and smashed into a paste with ½ tsp. salt

MAKE AHEAD:
Stuffed Jalapeños can be made through step #7 up to 2 days ahead of baking and serving. Keep covered and refrigerated.

Directions

1. Wash the peppers and cut them in half lengthwise. Try to split each pepper so that each half has a length of stem for eaters to use as a handle.
2. Wear plastic, food-safe gloves, or slip your hands into plastic food-safe baggies, and use your covered fingers to remove the seeds and membranes from inside the pepper halves, leaving the stem intact. Discard the seeds and membranes. Do not attempt this without the protection of gloves. Hot peppers contain capsaicin, which can cause a burning sensation on your skin that persists for hours (or longer ...).
3. Place pepper halves on a baking sheet, open side up.
4. Preheat oven to 375°.
5. In a medium mixing bowl, soften the cream cheese by smushing it with a strong spatula or spoon.
6. Add remaining filling ingredients to the bowl. Mix the ingredients thoroughly.
7. Fill the cavity of each pepper with filling, pressing the filling down into all the nooks and crannies. Use up all of the filling, distributing it evenly.
8. Bake peppers for 45 minutes.
9. Transfer peppers to a serving platter and serve warm.

MOLÉ BROWNIES

Makes 9" x 13" pan

The combination of sweet and spice in these fudgy brownies is extraordinary! They will turn out no matter what brand of chocolate and cocoa you use, but I must tell you that quality matters. Better quality chocolate = better quality brownies.

Ingredients

- 1 cup butter (2 sticks)
- 6 oz. dark chocolate or 1 cup semi-sweet chocolate chips
- ½ cup Dutch-processed baking cocoa
- 1 tsp. instant coffee or espresso powder
- 4 oz. cream cheese, at room temperature (½ of an 8 oz. block)
- 2 cups granulated sugar
- 4 large eggs
- 1 Tbsp. vanilla extract
- ½ cup all-purpose flour
- 2 tsp. ground cinnamon
- 1 tsp. chili powder
- 1 tsp. ground chipotle pepper
- ½ tsp. salt
- ¼ tsp. ground cloves

Directions

1. Preheat oven to 350°.
2. Grease a 9" x 13" baking pan. Set aside.
3. In a 2-quart saucepan over medium-low heat, melt the butter, chocolate, cocoa, and coffee. Stir almost constantly. When melted, remove from heat.
4. Add cream cheese and sugar to mixture in pan. Stir in.
5. Add eggs, one at a time, stirring quickly and vigorously after each addition (to keep the eggs from scrambling in the warm mixture). Add the vanilla with the final egg.
6. Add the remaining ingredients. Stir just until no white blotches of flour remain.
7. Spread batter in prepared pan.
8. Bake brownies for 35 minutes.
9. Remove brownies from oven and allow to cool completely before cutting into 48 squares.

MAKE AHEAD:
Molé Brownies can be made up to 3 days ahead of serving. Keep tightly covered at room temperature. Cut just before serving.

VEGETARIAN

RAJAS CON QUESO DIP

Makes 6 cups

Mild, creamy, complex, and tremendously delicious, partygoers will scrape this bowl clean. Don't substitute queso blanco or queso fresco cheese for the pepper Jack, as they aren't melty enough for this. And I know, rajas means "ropes" and this recipe calls for the peppers to be diced, not sliced, but we're not going to talk about that, okay?

Ingredients

Dip:

- 6 large poblano chile peppers
- 8 oz. block cream cheese, at room temperature
- ½ cup ricotta cheese
- 1 cup frozen sweet corn
- 1 cup finely diced white or yellow onion (1 medium onion)
- 1 Tbsp. minced garlic (3 large cloves), smashed into a paste with 1 tsp. salt
- 2 cups shredded pepper Jack cheese (8 oz.)
- ½ tsp. ground black pepper

Serving:

- 8 oz. bag tortilla chips

MAKE AHEAD:
Rajas Con Queso Dip can be made through step #8 up to 2 days ahead of baking and serving. Keep covered and refrigerated.

Directions

1. **For dip:** Preheat oven broiler to high. Move oven rack into the highest position.
2. Place peppers directly on oven rack. Roast peppers for 5–10 minutes on each of four sides. Peppers should be blistered and blackened on all sides.
3. Remove peppers from oven and place them either in a plastic bag or a covered bowl. Allow peppers to steam for at least 5 minutes.
4. While peppers are steaming, place cream cheese and ricotta in a large mixing bowl. Mix until thoroughly combined.
5. When peppers are done steaming, remove skins, seeds, and stems from peppers (do your best, but there's no need to be perfect with this).
6. Cut peppers into ¼" dice and add to the cream cheese mixture.
7. Add remaining dip ingredients to bowl. Stir to combine.
8. Transfer dip to a 2-quart baking dish.
9. Reduce oven temperature to 350°. Move rack to center of oven. Bake dip for 30 minutes, until mixture is hot and bubbly.
10. Serve dip hot with tortilla chips on the side for scooping.

VEGETARIAN

QUESADILLAS

Makes 48 appetizer triangles

Quesadillas are essentially Mexican grilled cheese sandwiches made with tortillas. Subject to endless improvisation and culinary creativity, I have a sister-in-law who asserts that you can make literally anything into a quesadilla—including leftover Chinese take-out. While I do not doubt her claim, I assert that cheese is essential for a successful quesadilla, as melted cheese acts as the glue that holds the whole thing together.

Ingredients

- 16 oz. package small corn tortillas (24 tortillas, 5 ½" diameter)
- 8 oz. shredded mozzarella cheese (2 cups) for mild heat; pepper Jack for more intense heat; and Cabot Creamery's habanero cheddar for face-melting heat
- 12 oz. package meatless veggie chorizo sausage (plastic casings removed, if present)
- 2 Tbsp. cilantro pesto (from recipe on next page), or 2 Tbsp. chopped fresh cilantro
- 3 Tbsp. vegetable or olive oil for frying

Serving:

- 8 oz. container sour cream (1 cup)
- 16 oz. jar salsa, your choice of type and heat level (2 cups)

Directions

1. If using Cilantro Pesto in this recipe, make that first (recipe on next page).
2. Place a heavy, 8" frying pan over medium heat (a cast iron pan works best) and allow it to heat while you assemble quesadillas.
3. Lay half of the tortillas out on a work surface.
4. Sprinkle cheese on each tortilla. Use up all the cheese and distribute it evenly.
5. Using hands, crumble chorizo over the cheese. Use up all the chorizo and distribute it evenly.
6. Spread a thin layer of Cilantro Pesto on each of the remaining tortillas. Top each "stack" with one of these tortillas, pesto side down. If using chopped cilantro, simply sprinkle it on top of the chorizo before topping with plain tortillas.
7. Press down gently on each quesadilla "sandwich."
8. Pour ½ tsp. oil into hot pan and swirl to coat bottom of pan with oil.
9. Add one assembled quesadilla to pan. Fry for about 1 minute (bottom tortilla will shrink slightly and be browned).
10. Using a pancake turner, flip quesadilla over. Fry for about 1 minute more.
11. Remove from pan and transfer to a cutting board.
12. Repeat cooking process with remaining quesadillas.
13. Cut cooked quesadillas in half and then in half again, yielding four wedges from each.
14. Transfer triangles to a platter and serve with salsa and sour cream on the side for dipping.

VEGETARIAN

Quesadillas

CILANTRO PESTO

Ingredients

- 2 cups fresh cilantro leaves and small stems (1 grocery store bunch)
- 3 large garlic cloves, sliced (1 Tbsp.)
- 1 jalapeño, seeded and roughly diced (leave seeds in for a hot pesto)
- ¼ cup sunflower seeds
- ½ tsp. ground cumin
- ¼ tsp. salt
- ½ cup sesame oil
- ¼ cup vegetable oil
- 1 Tbsp. lime juice (½ of a lime)
- ½ cup grated asiago cheese (2 oz.)

Directions

1. In container of blender or food processor, dump all ingredients except cheese.
2. Pulse mixture a few times to begin to chop leaves. Pack cilantro leaves down in-between pulsings.
3. Once mixture begins to blend and move in machine, process it on high until cilantro is ground very finely and the mixture is emulsified.
4. Add cheese and pulse a few times to mix in.
5. Taste, and adjust seasoning. Transfer pesto to a covered container and refrigerate.

MAKE AHEAD:
Cilantro Pesto will keep for 5–7 days in the refrigerator, but can be made up to 6 months ahead of serving, if frozen. Freeze pesto in an ice cube tray. Transfer frozen cubes to a ziptop bag and remove them to thaw as needed.

VEGAN

CHIPOTLE FISH FRITTERS

Makes 36 one-and-a-half inch fritters

Choose your preferred heat level when you make these unusual, fried balls of addictive goodness! Sort of like a spicy hush puppy, the mix of corny goodness with veggie bacon, smoky chipotle peppers and mild fish is perfection!

--- Ingredients ---

Oil:

- 8 cups vegetable oil for deep frying (64 oz.)

Batter:

- 1 ½ cup instant corn Masa flour (for making tortillas) or cornmeal
- ½ cup all-purpose flour
- 2 Tbsp. granulated sugar
- 2 tsp. baking powder
- 1 tsp. salt
- 1 tsp. onion powder
- ½ tsp. baking soda
- 2 large eggs
- 1 cup buttermilk (or ½ cup sour cream + ½ cup milk)
- 4 oz. can diced, roasted green chile peppers
- ½ cup frozen corn
- 1 tsp. (for mild) to 1 Tbsp. (for spicy) chipotle peppers in adobo sauce, finely minced (4 oz. can = 4 Tbsp.; chop and freeze the rest of the can for later use)

Meat:

- 1 lb. whitefish filets (tilapia, cod, flounder, or other), cut in ½" dice
- 6 oz. package smoky tempeh or other veggie bacon, diced

SEAFOOD

Directions

1. **For frying:** In a stockpot, deep frying pan, electric fryer, or wok, heat oil to 350° (a deep-fry thermometer is invaluable). Oil should be at least 3" deep. Line a baking sheet with several layers of paper towels or newspaper, lay a cooling rack upside down on top of paper, and set aside. While oil is heating, mix up batter.
2. **For batter:** In a large mixing bowl, combine dry ingredients. Stir until mixed.
3. Add eggs, buttermilk, peppers, corn, and chipotle. Stir just until blended.
4. Add fish and tempeh. Gently fold in.
5. When oil is up to temperature, drop 1 ½ tablespoon-sized balls of batter into oil (a 1 oz. cookie scoop works great for this). Do not crowd the pot—cook the fritters in batches, as needed. Cook each batch for 5–6 minutes total, flipping them over as needed for even browning.
6. Remove fritters with tongs or a kitchen spider and lay on prepared tray to drain. Allow oil to come back up to temperature before adding next batch of batter.
7. Transfer finished fish fritters to a platter or large bowl and serve hot.

MAKE AHEAD:
Chipotle Fish Fritters can be made ahead of serving—up to 4 days ahead if refrigerated, and up to 3 months ahead if frozen. Thaw and re-heat on a baking sheet in a 300° oven for 10 minutes.

FISH TACOS
Makes 24 mini tacos

If you have the setup to grill the fish for this dish and want that extra layer of flavor, go for it. But for the rest of us, these tacos are tremendously tasty with "just" baked fish as described. Classic street taco style with a distinctive slaw, these tacos are the ultimate finger food.

--- Ingredients ---

Slaw:

- 16 oz. bag coleslaw mix (or 4 cups shredded green cabbage + 2 cups shredded carrots)
- 1 cup shredded radishes (1 grocery store bunch; 8 oz.)
- 4 oz. can diced, mild green chile peppers
- 2 Tbsp. fresh cilantro, minced
- ¼ cup mayonnaise
- ¼ cup sour cream
- zest and juice of 2 limes (4 tsp. zest + 4 Tbsp. juice)
- 1 tsp. salt

Fish:

- 2 lbs. raw whitefish filets (tilapia, cod, haddock, or other)
- 1 Tbsp. taco seasoning (store-bought packet 1 oz. = 3.5 Tbsp., or homemade from recipe on next page)
- spray oil

Tortillas:

- two 11 oz. packages mini flour tortillas (24 street taco tortillas)

Spread:

- ½ cup Sriracha mayonnaise (store-bought or ½ cup mayo + ¾ tsp. Sriracha hot sauce)

Directions

1. **For slaw:** In a large mixing bowl, combine all ingredients for slaw. Stir until veggies are evenly coated and seasonings are evenly distributed.
2. Transfer slaw to a covered container and refrigerate for at least 24 hours.
3. **For fish:** Preheat oven to 350°.
4. Lay fish out on a greased baking sheet in a single layer, skin side down.
5. Sprinkle taco seasoning evenly over fish. Spray seasoned fish with oil.
6. Bake fish for 10 minutes per inch of thickness.
7. **For shells:** Remove tortillas from packages. Wrap in paper towels for heating in the microwave or in aluminum foil for heating in the oven. Heat tortillas.
8. **To assemble:** Place slaw in a colander set in a bowl. Allow excess liquid to drain off slaw (discard liquid).
9. Into two 9" square baking pans (or the equivalent) set up the tortillas as taco shells. Gently fold the tortillas in half and line them up, open side up, in two rows in each of the pans.
10. Into each tortilla, spread 1 teaspoon Sriracha mayo.
11. In the bottom of each tortilla scoop about ¼ cup slaw. Divide the slaw evenly and use it all up.
12. Top the slaw with a generous ounce of fish per taco. Divide the fish evenly and use it all up.
13. Serve fish tacos immediately.

MAKE AHEAD:
The slaw for Fish Tacos must be made one day ahead of serving.

TACO SEASONING
Makes 7 tablespoons (equal to two packets)

Full-flavored without all the additives that store-bought packets of seasoning contain, this is well worth the few minutes it takes to make.

Ingredients

- 2 Tbsp. chili powder
- 1 Tbsp. onion powder
- 1 Tbsp. ground cumin
- 1 Tbsp. salt
- 2 tsp. paprika (sweet, hot, or smoked—your choice)
- 1 tsp. garlic powder
- 1 tsp. dried oregano
- 1 tsp. ground black pepper
- ½ tsp. ground coriander
- ¼ tsp. cayenne pepper (omit if making this for children)

Directions

1. In a small bowl, combine all ingredients and mix with a whisk.
2. Transfer mixture to a spice jar or other airtight container. Label with: 3 ½ Tbsp. seasons 1 lb. meat or plant-based meat alternative.

MAKE AHEAD:
Taco Seasoning will maintain its flavor for a year at room temperature and longer if stored in the freezer.

EMPANADAS ("MEAT" PIES)

Makes 32 four-inch pies

The list of ingredients used to fill these empanadas sounds a bit unusual, but I swear on all that is holy that they are incredible, and will be the talk of your party. You will need to plan ahead for the making of these—grocery store plantains are typically unripe, and can take up to two weeks to fully ripen (leave laying around at room temperature). And ripe plantains are essential for the correct flavor and texture in these empanadas. I am not the best with timing, so I like to keep a pair of ripe, mashed plantains in my freezer, always ready for an empanada craving. I knew you would ask, so I tried making these with ripe bananas in place of the plantains. The flavor was terrible and the texture was weird, so please don't substitute.

Ingredients

Crust:

- 3 cups masa flour (as for tortillas)
- 1 ½ cups all-purpose flour
- 2 Tbsp. paprika (sweet, hot, or smoked)
- 1 ½ Tbsp. baking powder
- 2 tsp. salt
- ¾ cup cold butter (1 ½ sticks)
- 2 cups hot milk (not boiling, just jacuzzi-hot)
- 2 egg yolks

Filling:

- 2 ripe plantains (blackening peels)
- 15 oz. can black beans, drained
- 8 oz. package tempeh, crumbled
- 4 oz. can diced, mild green chile peppers
- ½ tsp. salt
- 16 oz. grated pepper Jack cheese (4 cups)

Egg Wash:

- 1 egg
- 1 Tbsp. milk

Serving:

- your choice of condiments for dipping: chipotle aioli (from recipe on next page), salsa, sour cream, and/or hot pepper sauce

Directions

1. **For crust:** In a medium mixing bowl, combine masa, flour, paprika, baking powder, and salt. Mix well.
2. Slice or dice butter and add to bowl. Using a pastry cutter or two forks, cut butter in until mixture resembles coarse crumbs. This can also be done in a food processor.
3. Add milk and egg yolks to bowl. Using clean hands, mix until a smooth dough forms. If dough is dry, add more milk, 1 tablespoon at a time, until dough is the consistency of stiff peanut butter. If dough is too sticky, add more flour, ¼ cup at a time.
4. Cover bowl with a damp towel. Set dough aside to rest while you prepare the filling.
5. **For filling:** In a large mixing bowl, place peeled plantains. Mash them with a potato masher until busted up but still a little chunky.
6. Add beans, tempeh, peppers, and salt. Stir until thoroughly combined.
7. Add cheese and mix in.
8. **To assemble:** Divide dough in half. Roll each portion of dough out to form a short snake. Cut each snake into 16 equal portions. Roll each portion into a ball.
9. Working with a few dough balls at a time (what your work surface will accommodate), roll each ball out to a 4" x 5" oval, using a rolling pin (do not flour work surface).
10. Top each oval with 1 ½ tablespoons of filling (a 1 oz. cookie scoop works great for this).
11. Fold dough in half, encasing filling. Press edges together. With the tines of a fork, crimp edge of pie to seal.
12. Place pies on a large, greased baking sheet and repeat process with remaining dough and filling.
13. Preheat oven to 375°.
14. In a mug or small bowl, combine egg and milk for egg wash. Brush tops of empanadas with this mixture.
15. Bake empanadas for 25–30 minutes, until lightly browned around the edges.
16. Serve empanadas warm, with condiments on the side for dipping.

MAKE AHEAD:
Empanadas can be made ahead of serving—up to 4 days ahead if refrigerated, and up to 3 months ahead if frozen. Thaw and re-heat on a baking sheet in a 300° oven for 10 minutes.

CHIPOTLE AIOLI
Makes 1 cup

The perfect accompaniment to Empanadas, this spicy aioli is great on many other things, including as a spread on sandwiches.

Ingredients

- 1 egg yolk (organic, if possible)
- 1 tsp. brown mustard
- ½ cup vegetable oil
- ¼ cup olive oil
- 1 small clove garlic (1 scant tsp.), minced and smashed to a paste with ¼ tsp. salt
- 1 Tbsp. chipotle peppers in adobo sauce, finely minced (¼ of a 4 oz. can —chop and freeze the rest of the can for a later use)
- 2 tsp. balsamic vinegar
- ½ tsp. ground coriander

Directions

1. In small bowl, whisk egg yolk and mustard together.
2. Dribble in small bits of oil at a time, whisking vigorously after each addition until all the oil is fully incorporated into the egg yolk mixture.
3. Add remaining ingredients and mix in.
4. Transfer aioli to a covered container and refrigerate. Aioli will keep for a month.

MAKE AHEAD:
Chipotle Aioli can be made up to 2 weeks ahead of serving.

GOING IT ALONE PARTY PREP COUNTDOWN

WEEKS BEFORE:
- ❏ Make "Meat"balls and freeze
- ❏ Make Chebureki and freeze
- ❏ Make Pumpkin Syrnyk and freeze

A WEEK BEFORE:
- ❏ Make Pickled Mushrooms
- ❏ Pickle beets for Canapés
- ❏ Make Cheesy Crackers
- ❏ Make horseradish sauce for Smoked Salmon on Rye

4 DAYS BEFORE:
- ❏ Make Cheese Dip
- ❏ Make Honey Dip for apples

3 DAYS BEFORE:
- ❏ Make Vodka Sauce for meatballs
- ❏ Make Oladyi pancakes

2 DAYS BEFORE:
- ❏ Make Goat Cheese topping for Canapés
- ❏ Make Polenta and Stuffed Onions

1 DAY BEFORE:
- ❏ Toast bread and roll salmon for Smoked Salmon on Rye
- ❏ Remove from freezer to thaw: "Meat"balls, Chebureki, Pumpkin Syrnyk

DAY OF PARTY:
Morning
- ❏ Set up food table with serving dishes
- ❏ Marinate tuna steaks
- ❏ Cut apple slices and soak

2 Hours Before Party
- ❏ Make Roasted Potatoes
- ❏ Make Egg Salad

45 Minutes Before Party
- ❏ Re-heat in oven: Chebureki, Polenta with Stuffed Onions
- ❏ Re-heat on stovetop: "Meat"balls & Sauce
- ❏ Assemble: Oladyi with Egg Salad, Pickled Beets, Smoked Salmon on Rye

15 Minutes Before Party
- ❏ Sear tuna, assemble Seared Tuna

UKRAINE

PARTY FOR 24

In taste tests and trials, this chapter was the most fun to present. Nobody wanted to eat anything. They took one look at the luscious spread, saw weirdness, and balked. "You expect me to eat beets?" "What's in that pinkish egg salad?" "Meatballs in vodka?"

I DID expect them to eat beets (and it's vodka sauce, Frank), but it was a hard sell. Inevitably, several someones in the group would go straight for the cheesecake. And then one brave soul (on a dare?) would try the Pickled Beet Canapés with Goat Cheese, or the Seared Tuna with Caviar, and compliments to the chef would follow. Soon, people were trying things they had never heard of (like Chebureki or the Cheese Dip with sardines in it), coming back for more, and engaging in lively banter about which dish was their favorite. Just what I was hoping for :~) FYI: This party has lots of canapés on the menu, and works best if you have help with final assembly during that last hour before guests arrive (or help from guests who love to pitch in).

APPLE SLICES AND HONEY DIP

Makes 2 cups dip

This dip is so simple and so good! And dipping the apple slices in honey water keeps them from browning, so you can slice them up several hours ahead of serving time.

Ingredients

Dip:

- 8 oz. brick cream cheese, at room temperature
- ¼ cup plain Greek yogurt
- ½ cup honey
- 1 tsp. ground cinnamon
- 1 tsp. vanilla extract
- ¼ tsp. salt

Apples:

- 6 tart apples (Granny Smith, Fuji, or other; no red delicious)
- 4 cups room temperature water
- 4 Tbsp. honey

Directions

1. **For dip:** In a small mixing bowl, combine all ingredients for dip. Whisk until smooth and homogenous. If not serving right away, cover and refrigerate.
2. **For apples:** Wash apples with soap and water to remove dirt and wax. Rinse well.
3. In a large mixing bowl, combine water and honey. Stir to dissolve honey.
4. Cut apples in quarters, remove cores, stems, and blossom ends. Cut quarters into slices. Immediately immerse apple slices in the honey water.
5. Gently stir apple slices to be sure they are all coated in honey water. Let soak for at least 5 minutes and up to 1 hour. Drain liquid off.
6. **To serve:** Transfer dip to a serving bowl. Set it on a platter or in a larger bowl, surrounded by apple slices.

MAKE AHEAD:

Honey Dip can be made up to 4 days ahead of serving. Keep covered and refrigerated.

ROASTED POTATOES

Makes 6 cups

In general, I don't consider chunks of potato an appetizer. But these work so well as part of a finger food buffet that I may have to change my tune. Crispy outside, tender inside, and seasoned just right, these are a delight.

Ingredients

- 2 lbs. russet or red potatoes, scrubbed (6 fist-sized spuds or 8 cups new potatoes)
- 3 large cloves garlic, finely minced or pressed (1 Tbsp.)
- ¼ cup olive oil
- 1 Tbsp. onion powder
- 1 tsp. caraway seeds
- 1 tsp. salt
- ½ tsp. dried thyme

Directions

1. Preheat oven to 425°.
2. Cut potatoes into 1" chunks, relatively even in size (leave small new potatoes whole). Place chunks in a 9" x 13" baking pan.
3. Pour oil over potatoes. Sprinkle remaining ingredients over potatoes. Mix well to distribute oil and seasonings evenly.
4. Roast potatoes for 50 minutes, stirring once in the middle of roasting time.
5. Transfer potatoes to a serving bowl. Serve hot or at room temperature with forked picks or toothpicks.

VEGAN

SMOKED SALMON ON RYE

Makes 30 canapés

Visually striking on a buffet, easy to make, and easy to manage when eating—what more could you want? Oh yeah—these gems are also incredibly delicious!

Ingredients

Horseradish Sauce:

- 1 to 4 Tbsp. prepared horseradish (brands vary)
- 3 Tbsp. sour cream
- 1 Tbsp. mayonnaise
- 1 Tbsp. snipped fresh chives or 2 tsp. dried chives
- 1 tsp. brown mustard
- ¼ tsp. granulated sugar
- ¼ tsp. salt
- ¼ tsp. ground black pepper

Canapés:

- 16 oz. loaf thin-sliced dense rye bread (as for canapés or finger sandwiches) or 8 oz. box rye crackers
- 12 oz. package nova or Scottish style cold-smoked salmon
- 1 Tbsp. snipped fresh chives or dried parsley

MAKE AHEAD:
Horseradish sauce can be made up to a week before serving. Keep covered and refrigerated. Rye bread can be toasted 1 day before serving. The smoked salmon can be cut and rolled 1 day before serving. Keep toast at room temperature and salmon in refrigerator. Assemble right before serving.

Directions

1. **For sauce:** In a small bowl, combine 1 tablespoon horseradish and all other sauce ingredients. Mix until thoroughly combined. Taste for horseradish intensity. If you wonder if it needs more, it needs more. Add more, a tablespoon at a time, until you have no doubts. Cover and refrigerate until needed.
2. **For canapés:** Toast rye bread until crispy. Cut in 2" squares or the equivalent triangles.
3. **To assemble:** Lay toasts out on a platter, in a single layer.
4. Top each toast with a ½ teaspoon dollop of horseradish sauce.
5. Rip each slice of salmon into pieces 2" to 3" long. Roll each piece up (will form a sort of rosebud shape). Lay one piece of salmon on each toast.
6. Sprinkle chives over top to garnish. Serve immediately.

SEAFOOD

SEARED TUNA WITH CAVIAR

Makes 30 appetizers

If you have a big mouth :~) you can pop one of these in whole. And with that first bite, the flavors will explode in your mouth to stimulate every taste bud, satisfy every craving. So good…. No way to get a sneak peek, though—these must be assembled at the last minute, as the crackers will start to soften after about an hour on a buffet.

Ingredients

Marinade:

- 1 Tbsp. lemon juice
- 2 Tbsp. olive oil
- 2 tsp. minced garlic (2 large cloves), smashed to a paste with ½ tsp. salt
- 1 Tbsp. minced fresh dill or 1 tsp. dried dill weed
- 2 tsp. dried rubbed sage
- 1 tsp. ground black pepper

Tuna:

- 12 oz. raw, thick-cut tuna steaks, cut in half to make generous 1" x 1" sticks
- 1 Tbsp. olive oil

Serving:

- 30 butter crackers (8 oz. box Ritz, Club, Town House, or other)
- 3 Tbsp. brown or Dijon-style mustard
- 1 cup sauerkraut, well-drained (½ of a 15 oz. can)
- 2 oz. jar salmon caviar

Directions

1. **For tuna:** In a quart ziptop bag, combine all ingredients for marinade. Close bag and agitate to mix.
2. Add tuna to bag. Close bag and manipulate tuna until all pieces are covered in marinade. Remove air from bag. Seal bag and refrigerate 30 minutes to 4 hours.
3. Heat an 8" cast iron skillet over medium-high heat.
4. When the pan is smoking hot, add the tablespoon of olive oil to pan and swirl to coat bottom. Working quickly, pull tuna pieces from the bag and place in the pan.
5. Sear tuna on first side for 30 seconds, flip, cook for 30 seconds more, then cook for 30 seconds on each of the remaining sides. DO NOT OVERCOOK TUNA. Remove tuna from pan and place on a plate.
6. Allow tuna to cool slightly, then cut across the sticks, making square-ish ¼" thick slices.
7. **To assemble:** Spread a light coating of mustard on each cracker.
8. Top each cracker with a good pinch of sauerkraut, slice of tuna, and tiny scoop of caviar (⅛ tsp.). Transfer to a serving platter and serve.

SEAFOOD

PUMPKIN SYRNYK (CHEESECAKES)

Makes 24 mini-cakes

Creamy, pumpkin-y, gently spiced, and easy to handle, these are the perfect dessert to cap off a wonderful party.

Ingredients

Crust:

- 24 paper or foil standard muffin cup liners
- 24 round gingersnap cookies (½ of a 14 oz. box; if you have a choice of brands, Stouffer's has best flavor, best size cookie)

Filling:

- 16 oz. tub 4% milkfat cottage cheese (2 cups)
- 15 oz. can solid-pack pumpkin puree (1 ¾ cups)
- 4 large eggs
- ¼ cup sour cream
- ¾ cup brown sugar
- 2 Tbsp. cornstarch
- 2 tsp. ground cinnamon
- ½ tsp. ground ginger
- ¼ tsp. ground cloves
- ¼ tsp. salt
- 1 tsp. vanilla extract

MAKE AHEAD:
Pumpkin Syrnyk can be made 1 day ahead of serving if refrigerated, and up to 3 months ahead if frozen. Keep in an airtight container and thaw before serving.

Directions

1. **For crust:** Place a paper liner in 24 cups of two standard muffin tins. Place a ginger snap cookie in the bottom of each liner, flat side down.
2. **For filling:** Preheat oven to 350°.
3. Into the container of a blender, dump all filling ingredients. Process on high until smooth, scraping down sides of container as needed.
4. Pour or spoon mixture into liner cups, on top of the cookies. Distribute filling evenly and use it all up.
5. Bake cheesecakes for 25 minutes, until the centers aren't liquidy (they will jiggle but not slosh).
6. Remove, allow cheesecakes to cool completely in the tin, then transfer them to a covered container and chill. Serve cold or at room temperature.

VEGETARIAN

CHEESE DIP

Makes 4 cups

Distinctive and unforgettable! This cheese dip is soft and scoop-able (no knife required), but packs a full-flavored wallop. Tangy, salty, creamy, and complex, it is quite the conversation-starter as party-goers try to figure out what is in it, and why they like it so much. And you can add this to the conversation: herring is a staple in the Ukrainian diet, and sardines are actually young herring.

Ingredients

Dip:

- 8 oz. cream cheese, at room temperature
- ¼ cup mayonnaise
- 5.75 oz. jar Spanish olives stuffed with pimientos, drained (1 heaping cup)
- 4 oz. tin sardines in oil (oil and all)
- 1 cup coarsely chopped red onion (½ large onion)
- 1 large clove garlic (1 tsp.)
- 1 Tbsp. Worcestershire sauce
- ¼ tsp. salt
- ⅛ tsp. ground black pepper
- 8 oz. shredded Bryndza cheese (2 cups) or crumbled feta cheese

Serving:

- 8 oz. box cheese crackers or homemade Cheesy Crackers from recipe on facing page

Directions

1. In the container of a blender or food processor fitted with a steel blade, combine all ingredients for the dip except the shredded cheese. Process on high until smooth.
2. Transfer mixture to a medium mixing bowl. Add shredded cheese and mix well.
3. Serve dip immediately.

MAKE AHEAD:
Cheese Dip can be made up to 4 days before serving. Keep covered and refrigerated.

SEAFOOD

CHEESY CRACKERS

Makes 6 cups of small, 1" crackers

I love Cheez-It crackers. There, I said it. But I dreamed of a homemade version that was EVEN BETTER. I headed into the kitchen thinking, "How hard can it be?" Turns out, it can be pretty hard. After several failed attempts with recipes I found on the internet, I bought a well-reviewed cracker cookbook, figuring that would do the trick. But no. Round after round of additional testing followed (so many crackers), and finally—picture me wiping sweat from my brow—I produced a cracker that makes me happy. So, so happy. I hope they make you feel the same.

Ingredients

- 1 cup all-purpose flour
- ½ cup whole wheat flour
- ½ cup grated Parmesan cheese
- ½ cup cheddar cheese powder (available from many retailers or sources online)
- 1 tsp. baking powder
- ½ tsp. salt
- 1 ¼ cups heavy cream

MAKE AHEAD:
Cheesy crackers can be made up to a week before serving. Store in an airtight container at room temperature.

Directions

1. Preheat oven to 300°.
2. In a small mixing bowl, combine the dry ingredients. Mix well.
3. Add the cream and blend in until the mixture forms a ball. The dough should be moist, hold together, and not be sticky. If crumbly, add a tablespoon of cream; if sticky add a few tablespoons of flour.
4. You will need two 14" x 18" baking sheets. Check the size of your baking sheets and gather an equivalent square footage. Line each with kitchen parchment or a silicone baking mat.
5. Divide the dough into portions appropriate for your baking sheets (into half, thirds, quarters, or irregular portions). Sprinkle a few tablespoons of all-purpose flour over the parchment/silicone mat and place the corresponding lump of dough on top. Sprinkle more flour over dough.
6. With a rolling pin, roll dough out until it is ⅛" thick, forming a rectangle on top of the parchment/silicone mat.
7. Cut dough into 1" squares and leave in place on paper. Prick each square in the center with a toothpick or bamboo skewer.
9. Bake crackers for 20 minutes. Crackers will rise and separate from one another during baking.
10. Flip crackers over on baking sheets and return to oven. Close door and turn oven off. Leave crackers in oven for 10 more minutes.
11. Remove crackers from oven. Press on center of crackers. Remove all crackers that are firm and allow them to cool. Return any crackers that are still soft to the oven (turned off) for 10 minutes more.
12. When all crackers are baked and cooled, transfer them to an airtight container and store them at room temperature.

VEGETARIAN

PICKLED MUSHROOMS
Makes 6 cups

Ukraine is known for its pickled vegetables. Here, mushrooms and roasted peppers join forces for a power-couple veggie dish.

Ingredients

Brine:
- 3 cups water
- 1 cup apple cider vinegar
- 1 Tbsp. prepared horseradish
- 2 tsp. salt
- 1 tsp. dry mustard powder

Vegetables:
- 4 large cloves garlic, finely minced or pressed (4 tsp.)
- 2 Tbsp. minced fresh dill or 2 tsp. dried dill weed
- 2 bay leaves
- 16 oz. fresh white mushrooms, baby bella portabella mushrooms, or a combination (6 cups)
- 16 oz. jar roasted red peppers, drained and cut in 1" pieces (2 cups)

Finishing:
- 2 Tbsp. olive oil

MAKE AHEAD:
Pickled Mushrooms must be made at least 2 days, and can be made up to two weeks before serving. Keep covered and refrigerated.

Directions

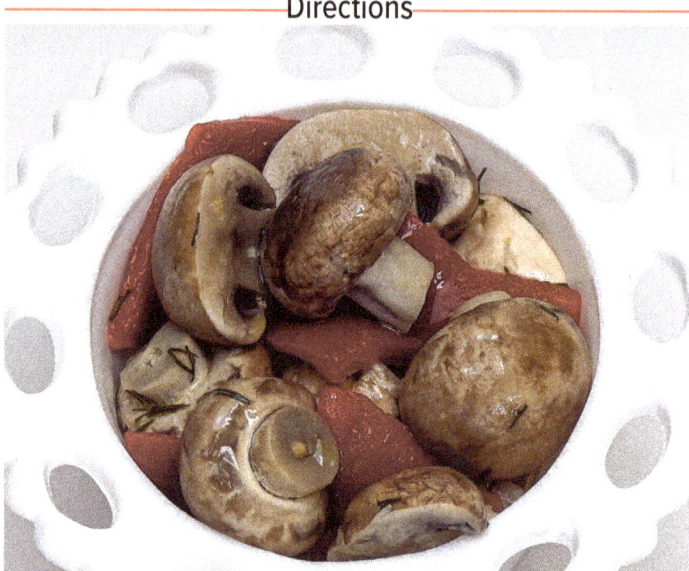

1. **For brine:** In a 2-quart pot, combine all brine ingredients. Cover pot.
2. Place pot over medium-high heat and bring to a boil. Reduce heat to low and simmer for 5 minutes.
3. **For vegetables:** Place garlic, dill, and bay leaves in a half-gallon glass jar (or divide into two quart jars).
4. Leave bite-sized mushrooms whole and cut others into halves or quarters, as needed. Layer mushrooms and peppers in glass jar(s). Tap jar bottom on your hand to settle the pieces in.
5. Pour hot brine over vegetables in jar(s). Screw on lid(s). Retain any extra brine, as the vegetables will settle and you will need that brine to top off the jar(s). Allow vegetables to sit until cooled to room temperature, then transfer to the refrigerator.
6. Allow vegetables to pickle for at least 2 days, and up to 2 weeks (refrigerated), agitating the jar(s) once a day.
7. **To serve:** Drain the pickling liquid off the vegetables. Transfer vegetables to a serving bowl and discard the bay leaves. Drizzle finishing oil over top and stir to incorporate. Serve vegetables cold or at room temperature, with fork picks or toothpicks.

PICKLED BEET CANAPÉS WITH GOAT CHEESE

Makes about 40 canapés of varied size

I dislike beets A LOT, so I worked on this recipe until I could not stop eating them. Trust me when I tell you that these are positively divine. Colorful, tasty, nutritious, and unusual, they require planning to pickle the beets, but very little time and effort overall.

Ingredients

Pickled Beets:

- two 15 oz. cans sliced beets, drained
- 1 cup apple cider vinegar
- ½ cup water
- ¼ cup granulated sugar
- 2 Tbsp. prepared horseradish
- 1 tsp. salt
- ½ tsp. dry mustard powder
- ¼ tsp. ground black pepper

Topping:

- 8 oz. fresh goat cheese
- 2 oz. bleu cheese, crumbled (½ cup)
- 2 Tbsp. mayonnaise
- 1 Tbsp. dried parsley
- ¼ tsp. ground black pepper

MAKE AHEAD:
Pickled Beets must be made at least 3 days ahead of serving, and can be made up to 4 weeks ahead. The Goat Cheese topping can be made up to 3 days ahead of serving. Keep everything covered and refrigerated. Assemble right before serving.

Directions

1. **For beets:** Transfer beet slices to a quart canning jar.
2. In a 1-quart saucepan, combine remaining ingredients for beets. Place pan over medium-high heat and bring to a boil.
3. Reduce heat to low and simmer mixture for 5 minutes. Remove from heat. Immediately pour mixture over beets. Cover jar and let beets sit for 24 hours at room temperature, then refrigerate them for at least 2 days.
4. **For topping:** In a medium mixing bowl, combine all topping ingredients. Mix just until everything is combined (over-mixing will cause the bleu cheese to turn everything green). Cover and refrigerate until needed.
5. **To assemble:** Drain beets. Lay slices out on paper towels to blot them dry.
6. Transfer beets to a serving platter, laid out in a single layer. Top each beet with a dollop of the cheese mixture. Serve canapés chilled or at room temperature.

POLENTA WITH STUFFED ONIONS

Makes 30 appetizers

I must confess that I didn't have much experience making or eating polenta before I started work on this cookbook. I know, I feel bad for me, too. Polenta is versatile and yummy, and I love that it cooks up firm enough to eat with your hands. Here, you can get by just fine with the pre-made stuff (which can be kind of bland), since the onions and sausage on top lend plenty of robust flavor to the finished appetizers.

Ingredients

Polenta:
- two 16 oz. packages heat-and-eat polenta
- 2 Tbsp. olive or vegetable oil

Onions:
- 3 to 4 three-inch diameter white or yellow onions

Filling:
- 12 oz. package veggie bulk sausage
- 8 oz. package horseradish cheddar cheese, shredded (2 cups)
- 1 Tbsp. dried parsley
- 1 Tbsp. vegetarian Worcestershire sauce

Topping:
- ½ cup sour cream

VEGETARIAN

Directions

1. **For polenta:** Remove polenta from packaging and cut in ¼" slices.
2. Brush oil on both sides of slices. Lay slices out on a baking sheet.
3. Heat oven broiler to HIGH and move oven rack to highest position.
4. Broil polenta slices for 10–15 minutes, until they are beginning to blister and brown. Flip slices over and broil 5–7 minutes more. Prepare onions while polenta is cooking.
5. **For onions:** Cut off both the top stems and bottom roots. Peel onions.
6. Cut each onion into ½" thick slices (3–4 slices per onion).
7. Separate the rings, gathering the ones that are 2" to 3" in diameter. Count until you have the same number of rings as you have polenta slices. Set aside the other onion rings for another purpose.
8. Lay the gathered rings out on a greased baking sheet.
9. When polenta is out of the oven, reduce oven temperature to 350°. Move oven rack back to the center position.
10. **For filling:** In a medium mixing bowl, combine all filling ingredients.
11. Stir or mix with hands until mixture is homogenous.
12. Using your hands, fill the inside each of the onion rings with the filling. Press the filling in, to eliminate air pockets.
13. Bake stuffed rings for 20 minutes.
14. Transfer cooked polenta slices to a serving platter. When onion rings are done, lay one on top of each slice of polenta. Top each with a dollop of sour cream. Serve immediately.

MAKE AHEAD:
Polenta with Stuffed Onions can be made through step #13 up to two days ahead of serving. Store polenta and onions separately in the refrigerator. Assemble and re-heat on a baking sheet in a 300° oven for 10 minutes, then top with sour cream.

OLADYI WITH EGG SALAD

Makes 45 two-and-a-half inch pancakes

Americans call these little buckwheat pancakes blini, but in Ukraine and neighboring parts of the world where they come from, they are called oladyi. Blini are actually like a French crêpe. Oladyi can be sweet, but here they are savory and paired with a classic Ukrainian egg salad, to spectacular result. The oladyi can be prepared ahead of time, but the egg salad is best served right after it is made.

Ingredients

Pancakes:

- 1 ¾ cups plain kefir (or 1 cup buttermilk + ¾ cup plain yogurt)
- 1 large egg
- 1 Tbsp. vegetable oil
- ¾ cup buckwheat flour
- ¼ cup all-purpose flour
- 1 Tbsp. granulated sugar
- ½ tsp. baking soda
- ¼ tsp. salt

Egg Salad:

- 5 hard-boiled eggs, cooled, peeled, and chopped
- 1 cup grated Emmentaler, Gouda, or smoked Gouda cheese (4 oz.)
- ½ cup sour cream
- ¼ cup mayonnaise
- 4 Tbsp. fresh snipped chives or 2 Tbsp. dried chives
- 1 tsp. paprika (sweet or smoked)
- ½ tsp. salt
- ¼ tsp. ground black pepper

> **MAKE AHEAD:**
> Oladyi pancakes can be made up to 3 days ahead of serving. Keep covered and refrigerated.

Directions

1. **For pancakes:** In a medium mixing bowl, whisk together kefir, egg, and oil.
2. Add remaining pancake ingredients and stir just until combined.
3. Place a griddle or large frying pan over medium-low heat (4 on a scale of 1 to 10). When pan is hot, either spray it with non-stick spray, or drizzle a teaspoon of oil in to coat the bottom.
4. Drop batter into pan in puddles that are 1 tablespoon of batter each. Space puddles 1" apart. Fry until bubbles pop on the surface of the pancakes and the edges look drier than the centers (about 2 minutes). Flip and cook a minute or two on the second side. Remove pancakes to a plate and repeat cooking process with remaining batter. When all pancakes are cooked, set them aside.
5. **For egg salad:** In a medium mixing bowl, combine all ingredients for egg salad. Stir gently until thoroughly mixed.
6. **To assemble:** Lay room temperature pancakes out on a serving platter. Top each with a half-tablespoon of egg salad. Serve immediately.

"MEAT" BALLS IN VODKA SAUCE

Makes 56 one-inch balls

These veggie meatballs are so full-flavored, and the sauce for them is so kicky, the combination is absolutely unbeatable.

--- Ingredients ---

Meatballs:

- 16 oz. package meatless ground beef (as for burgers)
- 14 oz. package meatless bulk sausage (no links or patties)
- 1 cup finely minced white or yellow onion (½ large onion)
- 1 cup grated carrots (2 large carrots)
- 1 Tbsp. finely minced or pressed garlic (3 large cloves)
- 1 cup dry bread or cracker crumbs
- ½ cup heavy cream or milk
- 1 egg
- 1 Tbsp. dried parsley
- 1 Tbsp. dried dill
- 1 Tbsp. paprika (sweet, hot, or smoked)
- ½ tsp. ground black pepper

Sauce:

- 2 Tbsp. olive oil
- 1 cup finely diced red onion (½ large onion)
- 1 Tbsp. finely minced or pressed garlic (3 large cloves)
- ½ cup vodka
- 15 oz. can tomato sauce (2 cups plain, not pasta sauce)
- 1 Tbsp. dried basil
- 2 tsp. dried oregano
- 1 tsp. salt
- ⅛ tsp. red pepper flakes
- ½ cup heavy cream

VEGETARIAN

Directions

1. **For meatballs:** Preheat oven to 400°. Grease a large baking sheet and set aside.
2. In a large mixing bowl, combine all ingredients for meatballs. Mix with hands until thoroughly combined.
3. Form mixture into tablespoon-sized balls (a ⅔ oz. cookie scoop works great for this) and place on prepared baking sheet, leaving ½" space between balls.
4. Bake meatballs for 20 minutes, until meatballs are firm and lightly browned. While meatballs bake, prepare sauce.
5. **For sauce:** In a 4-quart stockpot, heat oil over medium heat.
6. When oil is hot, add onions and garlic. Sauté until the onions are translucent (5 minutes). Add the vodka and stir, scraping any bits off the bottom of the pan.
7. When the vodka boils, add the tomato sauce and seasonings. Stir, cover, and allow sauce to simmer for 5 minutes.
8. Add cream to sauce. Stir in. Heat to a simmer, then turn burner off. Leave pan on burner to stay warm.
9. Add cooked meatballs to sauce in pan. Gently stir to coat meatballs in sauce.
10. Transfer meatballs to a serving bowl. Serve with fork picks or toothpicks.

MAKE AHEAD:
Meatballs can be made through step #4 up to 5 days ahead of serving if refrigerated, or up to 6 months ahead if frozen. Sauce can be made up to 3 days ahead of serving. Keep refrigerated. Thaw meatballs before adding to sauce. Simmer sauce and meatballs together for 10 minutes to re-heat.

CHEBUREKI ("MEAT" PIES)

Makes 24 four-inch pies

Chebureki are little meat pies sort of like empanadas, but with a very different flavor profile. Where empanadas are spicy and cheesy, chebureki are meaty and juicy.

--- Ingredients ---

Dough:

- 2 cups all-purpose flour
- 1 cup whole wheat flour
- 1 teaspoon salt
- 1 large egg
- ¾ cup warm water
- 1 Tbsp. vodka or apple cider vinegar

Frying:

- 1 to 2 cups vegetable oil

Filling:

- 12 oz. package meatless ground beef (as for burgers)
- ½ cup sour cream
- 1 cup finely minced white or yellow onion (½ large onion)
- 1 tsp. finely minced or pressed garlic (1 large clove)
- 2 Tbsp. dried parsley
- 3 Tbsp. minced fresh dill or 1 Tbsp. dried dill weed
- 1 tsp. salt
- ½ tsp. ground black pepper

Directions

1. **For dough:** In a medium mixing bowl, combine flours and salt. Mix well.

2. Add egg, water, and vodka. Mix with hands until mixture comes together to form a dough. Dough should be stiff and smooth. If dough is crumbly, add more water 1 tablespoon at a time. If dough is sticky, add flour 2 tablespoons at a time.

3. Set dough aside and flip bowl over to cover it. Let dough rest while you prepare the filling.

4. **For filling:** In a medium mixing bowl, combine all filling ingredients. Mix well.

5. **To assemble:** Roll dough into a snake and cut into 24 equal pieces. Roll pieces into balls.

6. Using a rolling pin, roll one portion of dough out to form a 4" x 5" oval.

7. Top dough with 1 ½ tablespoons filling (a 1 oz. cookie scoop works great for this). Leaving ¼" border around outside, spread filling out to cover half of disc.

8. Fold dough in half, with the filling inside. Press edges together. With the tines of a fork, crimp edge of pie to seal. Flip pie over and crimp other side.

9. Set pie aside and repeat process with remaining dough and filling.

10. **For frying:** In a large, broad frying pan, heat ½" oil over medium heat.

11. When oil is hot (should feel hot when hand is held 3" above it), add as many pies as will fit in a single layer in the pan. Fry until golden brown (about 2 minutes), flip, and fry until browned on second side. Transfer cooked pies to a paper towel-lined plate to blot off excess oil, then move them onto a serving platter.

12. Replenish oil as needed and fry remaining pies. Serve chebureki hot.

MAKE AHEAD:
Chebureki can be made ahead of serving—up to 4 days ahead if refrigerated, and up to 3 months ahead if frozen. Thaw and re-heat on a baking sheet in a 300° oven for 10 minutes.

GOING IT ALONE PARTY PREP COUNTDOWN

WEEKS BEFORE:
- ❏ Prep Buffalo Chik'N Dip and freeze
- ❏ Make Shrimp-Corn Fritters and freeze
- ❏ Make Potato Balls and freeze

A WEEK BEFORE:
- ❏ Make Ranch Dip

4 DAYS BEFORE:
- ❏ Make Rocky Road 7-Layer Cookies

3 DAYS BEFORE:
- ❏ Make Honey-Mustard Pecans
- ❏ Marinate mozzarella for BLT and C Skewers
- ❏ Make bacon mayonnaise for BLT and C Skewers

2 DAYS BEFORE:
- ❏ Prep burger mix for Mushroom-Blue Cheese Sliders (do not cook)
- ❏ Make mushroom topping for Sliders

1 DAY BEFORE:
- ❏ Make Mini Chicago-Style Deep Dish Pizzas
- ❏ Remove from freezer to thaw: Buffalo Chik'N Dip, Shrimp-Corn Fritters, Potato Balls

DAY OF PARTY:
Morning
- ❏ Set up food table and choose platters, bowls, and trays for serving all dishes
- ❏ Prep fresh vegetables and refrigerate
- ❏ Assemble BLT and C Skewers and refrigerate

2 Hours Before Party
- ❏ Make PB&J Turnovers
- ❏ Make Mushroom-Blue Cheese Sliders

45 Minutes Before Party
- ❏ Bake Buffalo Chik'N Dip
- ❏ Re-heat in oven: Shrimp-Corn Fritters, Potato Balls, Mini Chicago-Style Deep Dish Pizzas

U.S.A.

PARTY FOR 18

I know, I know … having a "United States" chapter in a cookbook that encourages Americans to be more adventurous in their cooking does seem wrong, somehow. But my thought was that if you are using this book to cook and party your way around the world with your friends or supper club, you really should launch or land in the United States. The foods here are familiar and kid-friendly, and this chapter is a safe place to start, to see if I know what I'm talking about. The menu presented here has something for everyone to love, with a combination of classics and twists on classics like Buffalo Chik'N Dip, Mushroom-Blue Cheese Sliders, Mini Chicago-Style Deep Dish Pizzas, and Rocky Road 7-Layer Cookies for dessert. The dishes complement one another in a companionable way, offering a delightful way to nosh your way through a big game, birthday party, 4th of July, family game night, or other casual gathering. If you will be making this whole chapter for a party, please add some fresh fruit to the line-up (like finger-food-friendly grapes, strawberries, sliced oranges, or other).

RANCH DIP WITH FRESH VEGGIES

Makes 3 cups dip

*This dip is nice and thick, so it won't be dripping all over everything at your party. * fist bump * Be sure to follow my advice and use a power tool to make it—made by hand, it will be tasty but lumpy.*

Ingredients

Dip:

- 8 oz. block cream cheese, at room temperature
- 1 cup mayonnaise
- ½ cup buttermilk
- 1 Tbsp. dried parsley
- 1 tsp. onion powder
- 1 tsp. garlic powder or 1 large clove garlic, minced and smashed to a paste with the salt
- 1 tsp. dill weed
- ½ tsp. salt

Veggies:

- 1 lb. baby carrots or carrot sticks
- 1 red, orange, or yellow bell pepper, seeded and cut top-to-bottom in narrow strips
- 1 cucumber, sliced
- 1 pint cherry tomatoes

Directions

1. **For dip:** In the bowl of a stand mixer with the beater attachment, or in a medium mixing bowl with a hand mixer, combine all ingredients for dip.
2. With the mixer on medium speed, beat ingredients until smooth and thoroughly combined.
3. Transfer dip to a serving bowl.
4. **To serve:** Arrange veggies on a serving platter around the bowl of dip.

MAKE AHEAD:
Ranch Dip can be prepared up to a week ahead of serving. Keep tightly covered and refrigerated.

U.S.A.

HONEY-MUSTARD PECANS
Makes 3 cups

Wowzers! These nuts pack an addictive punch! Sweet with a hint of heat from the mustard, the combination of flavors is game-day perfect. This recipe cooks up very quickly, so have all the ingredients at hand before you begin. And if you want to make these vegan, simply use vegetable oil instead of butter.

Ingredients

Spice Mix:

- 2 Tbsp. Colman's mustard powder
- 2 Tbsp. light brown sugar (packed)
- 1 tsp. onion powder
- ½ tsp. salt
- ¼ tsp. garlic powder
- ¼ tsp. paprika (sweet or hot)

Nuts:

- 1 Tbsp. butter
- 4 Tbsp. honey
- 16 oz. package raw pecan halves (3 heaping cups)

Directions

1. In a ramekin or mug, combine ingredients for spice mix. Stir to combine and bust up any lumps. Set next to cooktop.
2. Place a 12" frying pan over medium heat.
3. When pan is hot, add butter and honey. Swirl pan as mixture melts.
4. Add nuts to pan. Stir to coat nuts in honey mixture.
5. Sprinkle spice mix over nuts and stir.
6. Cook, stirring constantly, until nuts are coated in seasoning. Continue cooking and stirring until coating is no longer dry and powdery-looking (about 2 minutes).
7. Transfer nuts to a serving bowl. Allow nuts to cool.

MAKE AHEAD:
Honey-Mustard Pecans can be prepared up to a week ahead of serving. Tightly cover the serving bowl and keep at room temperature.

VEGETARIAN

PB&J TURNOVERS

Makes 18 - 20 appetizer pies

During testing, I tried making these buggers every which-way I could think of, with every conceivable combination of peanut butter and/or jams and/or fruits. Once I found the winning combination, I made them some more to get ratios just right. For lots of reasons, please trust me on this one! They are so simple, but truly cookbook-worthy! And they can be made vegan if you use a vegan puff pastry.

Ingredients

- 16 oz. package puff pastry, thawed and chilled
- 1 cup natural peanut butter (12 oz.)
- 1 cup strawberry or raspberry jam (8 oz.)
- 2 large or 3 small ripe bananas

Directions

1. Preheat oven to 425°.
2. Remove puff pastry from package and place sheet(s) on a clean, floured work surface.
3. Unfold puff pastry. With a rolling pin, gently roll out sheet(s). If package contains one sheet of puff pastry, the sheet should measure 18" x 14" and be cut into 20 squares (5 columns by 4 rows). If package contains two sheets of puff pastry, roll each sheet to 11" x 11" and cut into 9 squares each (3 columns by 3 rows).
4. Top each square with 2 teaspoons of peanut butter. Gently press each peanut butter glob into a rough triangle shape, on one diagonal half of the pastry square, staying ½" in from the edges.
5. Top each peanut butter triangle with 2 teaspoons jam.
6. Peel bananas. Stab a finger into the end of each, to split bananas into three long sticks. Cut each stick in half lengthwise to make 6 sticks, then crosswise in a small dice.
7. Top each PB pile with about a tablespoon of banana cubes. Distribute bananas evenly, and use them up.
8. Fold each pastry square in half on the diagonal, forming a triangle. Pinch the open edges shut.
9. Transfer pastries to a greased baking sheet.
10. Bake pastries for 15–20 minutes, until golden brown. Transfer to a serving plate and serve warm or at room temperature.

BUFFALO CHIK'N DIP

Makes 4 cups dip

Spicy, creamy, chunky, cheesy—this dip has it all! Inspired by buffalo wings, but without the mess that requires a million wet wipes and bibs, this dip will actually get invited back!

Ingredients

Dip:

- 8 oz. brick cream cheese, at room temperature
- ½ cup ricotta cheese (4 oz.)
- 1 red bell pepper, seeded and roughly chopped (1 cup)
- 1 cup roughly chopped red onion (½ large onion)
- 2 large cloves garlic (2 tsp.)
- ½ cup hot pepper sauce (Frank's Red Hot, or another of your choice)
- ½ tsp. salt
- ¼ tsp. ground black pepper
- 8 oz. shredded pepper Jack cheese (2 cups; for milder dip use Monterey Jack cheese)
- two 10 oz. packages meatless diced chik'n (no need to thaw)

Topping:

- 1 cup bleu cheese crumbles (4 oz.)

Serving:

- 12 to 16 oz. bag sour cream & onion potato chips

Directions

1. Preheat oven to 350°.
2. **For dip:** In the container of a blender or food processor fitted with a steel blade, combine all ingredients for dip except the Jack cheese and chik'n. Process on high until veggies are tiny bits and mixture is smooth.
3. Transfer cheese mixture to a medium mixing bowl. Add shredded cheese and chik'n. Stir until well blended.
4. Transfer mixture to a 2-quart baking dish. Sprinkle bleu cheese on top.
5. Bake dip (uncovered) for 40–50 minutes, until bubbly and lightly browned on top. Remove from oven. Serve dip hot with a spoon in it and chips on the side.

MAKE AHEAD:
Buffalo Chik'n Dip can be prepared through step #4 ahead of time. Cover and refrigerate dip up to 4 days or freeze up to 3 months before thawing, baking, and serving.

ROCKY ROAD 7-LAYER COOKIES

Makes 9" x 13" pan

These are so abundantly, outrageously decadent, I worry about people who lack self-control. Seriously, these things could, like, kill somebody. You know, with sugar-coma level happiness.

Ingredients

Crust:

- ½ cup butter, melted (1 stick)
- 1 ½ cups Nilla Wafer crumbs (4 cups cookies)

Toppings:

- 1 cup chopped pecans or walnuts
- 1 cup milk chocolate chips
- 1 ½ cups broken Nilla Wafer cookies (the remainder of an 11 oz. box, crushed with hands)
- 1 ½ cups roasted, salted peanuts (remove any skins)
- 1 cup semi-sweet chocolate chips
- 2 cups vegetarian mini-marshmallows (about 4 oz.)
- 14 oz. can sweetened, condensed milk

MAKE AHEAD:
Rocky Road 7-Layer Cookies can be made up to 5 days ahead of serving. Keep tightly covered at room temperature. Cut cookies just before serving.

Directions

1. Preheat oven to 350°.
2. **For crust:** Melt butter in the microwave or on the stovetop. Blitz cookies in a blender or food processor to produce crumbs. Add crumbs to butter and stir until crumbs are an even color.
3. Scatter crumb mixture in the bottom of a 9" x 13" baking pan. Press mixture down to form an even crust.
4. One at a time, in the order listed, scatter the topping ingredients in even layers across the crust. The condensed milk should be drizzled over the top so as to cover everything.
5. Bake cookies for 25 – 30 minutes, until golden brown on top.
6. Remove from oven and allow to cool completely. Cut into 48 squares and serve.

VEGETARIAN

BLT AND C SKEWERS

Makes 60 appetizer skewers

BLT and C?!? Why yes, what you have here is an amped-up bacon-lettuce-tomato combo with marinated fresh mozzarella cheese. It is a deconstructed-reconstructed marvel with the lettuce, tomato, and cheese elements skewered for easy eating, to be dipped with wild abandon in the accompanying bacon mayo. Heaven!

Ingredients

Marinated Mozzarella:

- 4 Tbsp. olive oil
- 1 Tbsp. balsamic vinegar
- 1 large clove garlic (1 tsp.), finely minced and smashed into a paste with ½ tsp. salt
- 1 Tbsp. snipped chives, fresh or dried
- 1 tsp. dried basil
- ½ tsp. dried parsley
- ¼ tsp. dried red pepper flakes
- 16 oz. fresh mozzarella balls or log cut in ¾" pieces

Bacon Mayonnaise:

- 2 Tbsp. olive oil
- 5 oz. package smoky tempeh or other veggie bacon
- 2 cups mayonnaise
- 2 large cloves garlic (2 tsp.), finely minced and smashed into a paste with ½ tsp. salt
- 1 tsp. lemon juice

Skewers:

- 60 sandwich picks or 4" skewers
- 1 pint grape tomatoes
- 1 small head iceberg lettuce, cut in wedges, then bite-sized chunks

Directions

1. **For mozzarella:** In a 4-cup container with a tight fitting lid, combine marinade ingredients. Stir with a fork to combine.
2. Add mozzarella to marinade. Seal container and gently shake to coat cheese in marinade. Refrigerate for at least 24 hours, stirring mixture once a day to marinate evenly.
3. **For mayo:** Place a large frying pan over medium heat. When the pan is hot, add the oil and the veggie bacon.
4. Cook bacon, flipping pieces over as needed, until they are browned on both sides. Remove pieces to a plate when they finish cooking. Do not drain bacon on paper towels.
5. Reserve any remaining cooking oil from the frying pan and allow it to cool.
6. When the bacon strips have cooled enough to handle, transfer them to a cutting board and chop them into tiny bits. You should have ¾–1 cup bits.
7. In a small mixing bowl, combine bacon bits, reserved oil, and remaining mayo ingredients. Stir until well blended. Transfer to a serving bowl. Cover and chill until serving time.
8. **To assemble:** Thread 1 tomato, 1 chunk of lettuce, and 1 ball/cube of cheese on each skewer. Stack skewers on a serving platter accompanied by the bowl of bacon mayo with a spoon in it.

MAKE AHEAD:
Marinated mozzarella must be made at least 1 day ahead of serving, and can be made up to 4 days ahead. Bacon mayo can be made up to 3 days ahead of serving. Keep everything covered and refrigerated.

MUSHROOM-BLUE CHEESE SLIDERS

Makes 24 mini-burgers

This combo of flavors really satisfies. The meatiness of the meatless beef + smoky veggie bacon + sharp blue cheese + earthy mushrooms + tangy horseradish mayo + soft dinner rolls = Burgers For The Win!

Ingredients

Burgers:

- 2 lbs. meatless ground beef (as for burgers)
- 5 oz. package smoky tempeh or other veggie bacon, finely minced
- 4 oz. blue cheese, crumbled (1 cup)
- 1 tsp. salt
- ¼ tsp. ground black pepper
- 2 Tbsp. olive oil

Topping:

- 2 Tbsp. olive oil
- 24 oz. sliced white mushrooms (9 cups)
- 2 Tbsp. vegetarian Worcestershire sauce
- ½ tsp. salt

Serving:

- 24 dinner rolls (two 16 oz. packages), cut horizontally to make buns
- ½ cup horseradish mayonnaise (½ cup mayo + 1 tsp. to 1 Tbsp. prepared horseradish—brands vary)

MAKE AHEAD:
The mushroom topping can be prepared up to 4 days ahead of serving. Keep refrigerated and re-heat before serving. The burger mixture can be prepared up to 3 days ahead of cooking and serving. Keep mixture refrigerated.

Directions

1. **For burgers:** In a medium mixing bowl, combine veggie beef, tempeh, cheese, salt, and pepper (a clean hand works great for this).
2. Divide burger mixture into 24 equal portions (3 tablespoon ice cream scoop each). Roll each portion into a ball and lay on a plate. Set aside.
3. **For topping:** Place a 12" frying pan over medium-high heat and add oil.
4. When pan and oil are hot, add mushrooms. Sauté mushrooms for 10 minutes, stirring occasionally.
5. Add Worcestershire sauce and salt to mushrooms. Cook, stirring occasionally, until mushrooms are fully cooked and moisture has evaporated (about 10 minutes more).
6. Transfer cooked mushrooms to a bowl and put pan back on heat.
7. Add oil for frying burgers to pan. Swirl to coat. Add burgers to pan, pressing them into patties the same diameter as the dinner rolls they will be served on.
8. Cook burgers until browned (about 5 minutes), flip, and cook 5 minutes more.
9. Lay dinner roll bottoms out on a serving platter. Top each with a scoop of mushrooms. Divide mushrooms equally and use them up.
10. Lay a burger on top of each mushroom pile. Top each burger with 1 teaspoon horseradish mayo.
11. Set dinner roll tops on and serve.

SHRIMP-CORN FRITTERS

Makes 48 one-and-a-half-inch fritters

These Shrimp-Corn Fritters and my old-fashioned mini corndogs were in a fight-to-the-death competition to make it into this chapter. I love a good corndog, but I gotta tell you, they lost big-time to these fritters. Light, crispy, and corny, these fritters absolutely won the day.

Ingredients

Frying:

- 8 cups vegetable oil for deep frying (64 oz.)

Batter:

- 1 ½ cups instant corn Masa flour (for tortillas) or cornmeal
- ½ cup all-purpose flour
- 2 Tbsp. granulated sugar
- 1 ½ tsp. baking powder
- 1 tsp. seasoned salt
- ½ tsp. baking soda
- 1 ½ cups frozen sweet corn
- ¼ finely minced white or yellow onion
- 1 cup buttermilk (or ½ cup sour cream + ⅔ cup milk)
- 2 large eggs
- 2 lbs. raw shrimp, peeled, deveined and cut in ¼" slices

MAKE AHEAD:
Shrimp-Corn Fritters can be made ahead of serving. Cover and refrigerate fritters up to 2 days or freeze for up to 3 months. Thaw and re-heat on a baking sheet in a 300° oven for 10 minutes.

SEAFOOD

Directions

1. **For frying:** In a stockpot, deep frying pan, electric fryer, or wok, heat oil to 350° (a deep-fry thermometer is invaluable). Oil should be at least 3" deep. Line a baking sheet with several layers of paper towels or newspaper, lay a cooling rack upside down on top of paper, and set aside.
2. **For batter:** While oil is heating, mix up batter.
3. In a medium mixing bowl, combine dry ingredients with corn and onion. Stir until well blended.
4. Add buttermilk and eggs and stir until combined. Do not over-mix or fritters will be tough.
5. Gently fold in shrimp.
6. When oil is up to temperature, drop 1 ½ tablespoon sized balls of batter into oil (a 1 oz. cookie scoop works great for this). Do not crowd the pot—cook the fritters in batches as needed.
7. Cook fritters for 5–6 minutes (until golden brown), turning them over as needed for even browning.
8. Remove fritters with tongs or a kitchen spider and lay on prepared tray to drain.
9. Allow oil to come back up to temperature before adding next batch of batter.
10. Transfer fritters to a serving bowl or platter and serve hot.

POTATO BALLS

Makes 36 one-inch balls

These Potato Balls are a gift from me, to me. I am a potato-head, and everyone who knows me knows that I love potato skins. Like, I REALLY love them. But I absolutely hate making them. So I set out to re-imagine the potato skin, with those same unctuous flavors, but without the time-consuming bother. These are the result, and I cannot describe the happiness they bring me. Oh, an important warning: even if tempted, don't increase the amount of cheese in these. If you do, they will lose their structural integrity when fried (disastrously messy).

Ingredients

Roasted Potatoes:

- 3 fist-sized raw potatoes, cut in ½" dice (unpeeled, 1 lb.)
- 1 large white or yellow onion, cut in ¼" dice (1 ½ cups)
- 5.5 oz. package smoky tempeh or other veggie bacon, diced
- 1 tsp. salt
- 2 Tbsp. olive oil

Balls:

- 14 oz. can potatoes, drained, or 1 ½ cups leftover mashed potatoes
- 2 large eggs
- 1 cup shredded sharp cheese (4 oz. cheddar, swiss, or other)

Frying:

- 8 cups vegetable oil for deep frying (64 oz.)

Directions

1. Preheat oven to 425°.
2. **For roasted potatoes:** Place raw potatoes, onions, tempeh, salt, and olive oil in an 8" square baking pan. Stir to coat everything in oil.
3. Roast potato mixture for 45 minutes, until potatoes are fork-tender. Stir mixture once or twice during roasting.
4. Transfer potato mixture to a large mixing bowl. Mash lightly with a potato masher, leaving some chunks of potato.
5. **For balls:** In the container of a blender or food processor fitted with a metal blade, dump the drained, canned potatoes and eggs. Puree until smooth.
6. Add the potato puree and cheese to the bowl of smashed potatoes. Stir to combine.
7. **For frying:** In a stockpot, deep frying pan, electric fryer, or wok, heat oil to 350° (a deep-fry thermometer is invaluable). Oil should be at least 3" deep. Line a baking sheet with several layers of paper towels or newspaper, lay a cooling rack upside down on top of paper, and set aside.
8. When oil is up to temperature, drop 1 tablespoon-sized balls of batter into oil (a ⅔ oz. cookie scoop works great for this). Do not crowd the pot—cook the balls in batches as needed. Cook each batch for 3–4 minutes total, flipping them over as needed for even browning. If some of the balls stick together during frying, leave them be and separate them after cooking (they will burst if separated during cooking).
9. Remove balls with tongs or a kitchen spider and lay on prepared tray to drain.
10. Allow oil to come back up to temperature before adding next batch of balls.
11. Transfer potato balls to a serving bowl or platter and serve hot.

MAKE AHEAD:
Potato Balls can be made ahead of serving. Cover and refrigerate Potato Balls up to 2 days or freeze for up to 3 months. Thaw and re-heat on a baking sheet in a 300° oven for 10 minutes.

VEGETARIAN

U.S.A.

MINI CHICAGO-STYLE DEEP DISH PIZZAS

Makes 24 three-inch pies

I've been making my homemade, from scratch, Chicago-style deep dish pizzas for a long, long time, and am appalled that I never thought to try miniaturizing them. Until now. Smack my forehead, they are spectacular! Marvelous! Such a convenient size to grab and gobble, I will be making these A LOT.

--- Ingredients ---

Crust:

- ½ cup milk warmed to 105°–115° (should feel like warm bath water)
- 1 packet active dry yeast (2 ¼ tsp.)
- ¼ cup olive oil
- ½ tsp. salt
- ½ cup corn meal
- 1 ½ cups bread flour

Toppings:

- 16 oz. grated mozzarella cheese (4 cups)
- 4 oz. package vegetarian pepperoni or 6 oz. bulk veggie breakfast sausage (no links or patties)
- 28 oz. can diced tomatoes, drained
- 1 large clove garlic, minced or pressed (1 tsp.)
- 1 tsp. dried basil

Directions

1. **For crust:** In a medium mixing bowl, combine warm milk and yeast. Stir with a sturdy wooden spoon and allow to sit for 5 minutes for yeast to dissolve.
2. Add remaining ingredients for crust. Mix until a smooth dough forms.
3. Transfer dough to work surface and knead for a couple minutes, until dough is smooth and elastic.
4. Return dough to bowl. Cover bowl with a damp towel and set aside to rise for at least 1 hour, and up to 4 hours.
5. **To assemble:** When dough is ready, punch it down to deflate it, roll it into a snake, and divide it into 24 equal portions.
6. With a rolling pin, roll each portion out to a 3 ½" disc. Press each disc into the cup of a standard muffin tin (two tins total) to form cups 1" deep.
7. Pierce each crust bottom three times with the tines of a fork (pricks about half an inch apart).
8. Preheat oven to 425°. Allow crusts to rise while oven heats. Do not place any toppings on crusts at this time.
9. In a small mixing bowl, combine drained tomatoes, garlic, and basil. Stir to combine. Set aside.
10. **To bake:** When oven is up to temperature, place crusts in oven and bake them for 5 minutes.
11. Remove crusts from oven and add toppings as quickly as you possibly can, in the order listed (cheese on the bottom, pepperoni next, tomatoes on top). Distribute toppings evenly. Crusts will be over-full, but will melt down with baking.
12. Return pizzas to the oven and bake an additional 15 minutes. When done, pizzas will be golden brown around the edges and crust will have pulled away from the sides of the cups a little bit. Transfer pizzas to a platter and serve hot.

MAKE AHEAD:
Mini Chicago-Style Deep Dish Pizzas can be made up to 2 days ahead of serving. Keep covered and refrigerated. Re-heat on a baking sheet in a 300° oven for 10 minutes.

INDEX

B

BREAD
Gougères, 67
"Ham" and Cheese Toasties, 14
Himbasha Bread, 44
Pão De Queijo (Cheese Bread), 18

C

CHEESE
BLT and C Skewers, 164
Buffalo Chik'n Dip, 162
Cheese Dip, 146
Cheese Plate with Socca, 58
Cheese Tart, 68
Cheesy Crackers, 147
Crab Rangoon Dip, 25
Gougères, 67
"Ham" and Cheese Toasties, 14
Lobster Thermidors, 69
Mediterranean Tuna Salad Cups, 77
Mini Chicago-Style Deep Dish Pizzas, 168
Mushroom-Blue Cheese Sliders, 165
Olive Tapenade with Feta, 76
Palak Paneer (Cheese Sticks), 96
Pão De Queijo (Cheese Bread), 18
Pickled Beet Canapés with Goat Cheese, 149
Pizza al Pesto Genovese, 108
Pizza Boscaiola (Sausage and Peppers), 116
Pizza Cinque Formaggi (5-Cheese), 118
Pizza Margherita, 109
Pizza di Patate (Potato), 112
Pizza Pugliese, 119
Pizza Vegetariana, 114
Quesadillas, 130
Rajas Con Queso Dip, 129
Spanakopita (Spinach Pies), 84
Stuffed Jalapeños, 127

CHEESE DIPS
Buffalo Chik'n Dip, 162
Cheese Dip, 146
Cheeze Dip, 41
Olive Tapenade with Feta, 76
Rajas con Queso Dip, 129

CREAM CHEESE
Avocado Dip, 126
Chocolate-Hazelnut Dip with Cookies & Fruit, 60
Crab Quiche Bites, 64
French Onion Dip with Fresh Vegetables, 59
Honey-Lemon Dip with Fruit, 73

CRAB
Crab Quiche Bites, 64
Crab Rangoon Dip, 25

D

DAIRY-FREE
Awaze Tofu, 45
Bang Bang Tofu, 26
Brazilian Pineapple, 12
Buticha (Hummus) with Fresh Veggies, 40
Cheeze Dip, 41
Cod Fritters with Skordalia, 79
Curried Shrimp, 92
"Doro" Wat Bites, 42
Fish Pakoras (Fritters), 93
Fish Skewers, 15
Fried Rice Balls, 34
Himbasha Bread, 44
Hummus with Fresh Vegetables, 74
Indian Peanut Dip with Fresh Vegetables, 91
Injera Dumplings, 50
Kolo Snack Mix, 48
Lentil Sambusa, 52
"Meat" Balls in Coconut Sauce, 46
Pickled Mushrooms, 148
Pineapple Sticks with Dip, 39

Pizza ai Frutti di Mare (Seafood), 111
Roasted Potatoes, 142
Samosas, 100
Shrimp and Sausage Skewers, 13
Shrimp Balls, 27
Shrimp Provençal, 57
Shrimp Salsa, 125
Shrimp Souvlaki, 75
Spiced Cashews, 89
Spiced Watermelon Skewers, 123
Spicy-Sweet Roasted Brazil Nuts, 11
Steamed Dumplings, 31
Vegan Peanut Butter Cookies, 43
Vegetable Tempura, 32
Veggie Skewers, 105

DESSERTS

Almond Cookies, 24
Baklava Thumbprint Cookies, 78
Brigadiero, 16
Chocolate-Hazelnut Dip with Cookies & Fruit, 60
Lemon-Ricotta Cake, 106
Mango Cupcakes, 95
Molé Brownies, 128
Pumpkin Syrnyk (Cheesecakes), 145
Rocky Road 7-Layer Cookies, 163
Sablé Breton Cookies, 61
Vegan Peanut Butter Cookies, 43

DIPPING SAUCES

Apricot Chutney, 94
Chipotle Aioli, 137
Cilantro Pesto, 131
Hot Mustard Sauce, 30
Italian Pizza Sauce, 115
Skordalia, 80
Sweet-and-Sour Sauce #1, 30
Sweet-and-Sour Sauce #2, 30
Toum, 80
Tzatziki Sauce, 80

E

EGGS

Beurre Blanc Deviled Eggs, 66
Fried Rice Balls, 34
Oladyi with Egg Salad, 151

F

FISH

Chipotle Fish Fritters, 132
Cod Fritters with Skordalia, 79
Fish Pakoras (Fritters), 93
Fish Skewers, 15
Fish Tacos, 134
Mediterranean Tuna Salad Cups, 77
Salmon Croquettes, 63
Seared Tuna with Caviar, 144
Smoked Salmon on Rye, 143
Smoked Salmon Spring Rolls, 23

FRUIT

Apple Slices and Honey Dip, 141
Apricot Chutney, 94
Brazilian Pineapple, 12
Chocolate-Hazelnut Dip with Cookies & Fruit, 60
Honey-Lemon Dip with Fruit, 73
Lemon-Ricotta Cake, 106
Mango Cupcakes, 95
Pineapple Sticks with Dip, 39
Spiced Watermelon Skewers, 123

G

GLUTEN-FREE

Apple Slices and Honey Dip, 141
Avocado Dip, 126
Beurre Blanc Deviled Eggs, 66
Brazilian Pineapple, 12
Buticha (Hummus) with Fresh Veggies, 40
Cheese Plate with Socca, 58
Curried Shrimp, 92
Fish Pakoras (Fritters), 93
French Onion Dip with Fresh Vegetables, 59
Honey-Lemon Dip with Fruit, 73
Honey-Mustard Pecans, 160
Hummus with Fresh Vegetables, 74
Pão De Queijo (Cheese Bread), 18
Pickled Beet Canapés with Goat Cheese, 149
Pickled Mushrooms, 148
Pineapple Sticks with Dip, 39
Rajas Con Queso Dip, 129
Ranch Dip with Fresh Veggies, 159
Roasted Potatoes, 142
Salsa Verde, 124
Shrimp Provençal, 57
Shrimp Salsa, 125
Shrimp Souvlaki, 75

Smoked Salmon Spring Rolls, 23
Spiced Cashews, 89
Spiced Watermelon Skewers, 123
Spicy-Sweet Roasted Brazil Nuts, 11
Veggie Skewers, 105

L
LOBSTER
Lobster Thermidors, 69

M
"MEAT" PIES
BBQ Char Siu Puffs, 29
Chebureki, 154
Empanadas, 136
Lentil Sambusa, 52
Pastel, 19
Samosas, 100

"MEAT" BALLS
"Meat" balls in Coconut Sauce, 46
"Meat" balls in Hoisin Sauce, 28
"Meat" balls in Vodka Sauce, 152
Quibe "Meat" Skewers, 17

N
NUTS
Almond Cookies, 24
Baklava Thumbprint Cookies, 78
Cheeze Dip, 41
Honey-Mustard Pecans, 160
Hummus with Fresh Vegetables, 74
Indian Peanut Dip with Fresh Vegetables, 91
Kolo Snack Mix, 48
Korma Tofu, 98
Rocky Road 7-Layer Cookies, 163
Spiced Cashews, 89
Spicy-Sweet Roasted Brazil Nuts, 11
Vegan Peanut Butter Cookies, 43

P
PIZZA CRUSTS
Napoletana Pizza Crust, 107
Romana Pizza Crust, 110
Siciliana Pizza Crust, 117

Q
QUICK AND EASY
Apple Slices and Honey Dip, 141
Brazilian Pineapple, 12
Buticha (Hummus) with Fresh Veggies, 40
Cheese Plate with Socca, 58
Cheeze Dip, 41
Curried Shrimp, 92
Dal Dip with Naan Chips, 90
Honey-Lemon Dip with Fruit, 73
Honey-Mustard Pecans, 160
Hummus with Fresh Vegetables, 74
Indian Peanut Dip with Fresh Vegetables, 91
Olive Tapenade with Feta, 76
PB&J Turnovers, 161
Pineapple Sticks with Dip, 39
Ranch Dip with Fresh Veggies, 159
Roasted Potatoes, 142
Salsa Verde, 124
Shrimp Provençal, 57
Shrimp Salsa, 125
Shrimp Souvlaki, 75
Smoked Salmon Spring Rolls, 23
Spiced Cashews, 89
Spiced Watermelon Skewers, 123
Spicy-Sweet Roasted Brazil Nuts, 11

S
SEAFOOD
Cheese Dip, 146
Cheese Tart, 46
Chipotle Fish Fritters, 132
Cod Fritters with Skordalia, 79
Crab Quiche Bites, 64
Crab Rangoon Dip, 25
Curried Shrimp, 92
Fish Pakoras (Fritters), 93
Fish Skewers, 15
Fish Tacos, 134
Lobster Thermidors, 69
Mediterranean Tuna Salad Cups, 77
Olive Tapenade with Feta, 76
Pizza Ai Frutti Di Mare (Seafood), 111
Salmon Croquettes, 63
Seared Tuna with Caviar, 144
Shrimp and Sausage Skewers, 13
Shrimp Balls, 27
Shrimp-Corn Fritters, 166
Shrimp Provençal, 57

Shrimp Salsa, 125
Shrimp Souvlaki, 75
Smoked Salmon on Rye, 143
Smoked Salmon Spring Rolls, 23

SEASONINGS
Berbere Seasoning, 47
Garam Masala, 89
Taco Seasoning, 135

SHRIMP
Curried Shrimp, 92
Pizza Ai Frutti Di Mare (Seafood), 111
Shrimp and Sausage Skewers, 13
Shrimp Balls, 27
Shrimp-Corn Fritters, 166
Shrimp Provençal, 57
Shrimp Salsa, 125
Shrimp Souvlaki, 75

SKEWERS
Fish Skewers, 15
Quibe "Meat" Skewers, 17
Shrimp and Sausage Skewers, 13
Shrimp Souvlaki, 75
Spiced Watermelon Skewers, 123
Veggie Skewers, 105

T

TOFU
Awaze Tofu, 45
Bang Bang Tofu, 26
BBQ Char Siu Puffs, 29
Cheeze Dip, 41
Korma Tofu, 98

V

VEGAN
Apricot Chutney, 94
Awaze Tofu, 45
Bang Bang Tofu, 26
Brazilian Pineapple, 12
Buticha (Hummus) with Fresh Veggies, 40
Cheeze Dip, 41
Cilantro Pesto, 131
Dal Dip with Naan Chips, 90
"Doro" Wat Bites, 42
Falafel Fritters, 81
Himbasha Bread, 44
Honey-Mustard Pecans, 160

Hot Mustard Sauce, 30
Hummus with Fresh Vegetables, 74
Indian Peanut Dip with Fresh Vegetables, 91
Injera Dumplings, 50
Italian Pizza Sauce, 115
Kolo Snack Mix, 48
Korma Tofu, 98
Lentil Sambusa, 52
"Meat" Balls in Coconut Sauce, 46
Napoletana Pizza Crust, 107
PB&J Turnovers, 161
Pickled Mushrooms, 148
Pineapple Sticks with Dip, 39
Roasted Potatoes, 142
Romana Pizza Crust, 110
Salsa Verde, 124
Samosas, 100
Siciliana Pizza Crust, 117
Spiced Cashews, 89
Spiced Watermelon Skewers, 123
Steamed Dumplings, 31
Sweet-and-Sour Sauce #1, 30
Sweet-and-Sour Sauce #2, 30
Vegan Peanut Butter Cookies, 43
Veggie Skewers, 105

VEGETABLES
Avocado Dip, 126
Buticha (Hummus) with Fresh Veggies, 40
Dal Dip with Naan Chips, 90
French Onion Dip with Fresh Vegetables, 59
Hummus with Fresh Vegetables, 74
Indian Peanut Dip with Fresh Vegetables, 91
Moussaka Tarts, 82
Mushroom-Blue Cheese Sliders, 165
Palak Paneer (Cheese Sticks), 96
Pickled Beet Canapés with Goat Cheese, 149
Pickled Mushrooms, 148
Potato Balls, 167
Rajas Con Queso Dip, 129
Ranch Dip with Fresh Veggies, 159
Roasted Potatoes, 142
Salsa Verde, 124
Spanakopita (Spinach Pies), 84
Stuffed Jalapeños, 127
Stuffed Mushrooms, 62
Vegetable Tempura, 32
Veggie Skewers, 105

VEGETARIAN

Avocado Dip, 126
BBQ Char Siu Puffs, 29
Beurre Blanc Deviled Eggs, 66
BLT and C Skewers, 164
Buffalo Chik'n Dip, 162
Buticha (Hummus) with Fresh Veggies, 40
Chebureki ("Meat" Pies), 154
Cheese Plate with Socca, 58
Cheese Tart, 68
Cheesy Crackers, 147
Dal Dip with Naan Chips, 90
Empanadas ("Meat" Pies), 136
French Onion Dip with Fresh Vegetables, 59
Fried Rice Balls, 34
Gougères, 67
"Ham" and Cheese Toasties, 14
Honey-Mustard Pecans, 160
"Meat" Balls in Hoisin Sauce, 28
"Meat" Balls in Vodka Sauce, 152
Mini Chicago-Style Deep Dish Pizzas, 168
Moussaka Tarts, 82
Mushroom-Blue Cheese Sliders, 165
Oladyi with Egg Salad, 151
Palak Paneer (Cheese Sticks), 96
Pão De Queijo (Cheese Bread), 18
Pastel ("Meat" Pies), 19
PB&J Turnovers, 161
Pickled Beet Canapés with Goat Cheese, 149
Pizza al Pesto Genovese, 108
Pizza Boscaiola (Sausage and Peppers), 116
Pizza Cinque Formaggi (5-Cheese), 118
Pizza di Patate (Potato), 112
Pizza Margherita, 109
Pizza Pugliese, 119
Pizza Vegetariana, 114
Polenta with Stuffed Onions, 150
Potato Balls, 167
Quesadillas, 130
Quibe "Meat" Skewers, 17
Rajas Con Queso Dip, 129
Sausages in Crêpes, 65
Spanakopita (Spinach Pies), 84
Spicy-Sweet Roasted Roasted Brazil Nuts, 11
Stuffed Jalapeños, 127
Stuffed Mushrooms, 62
Vegetable Tempura, 32

www.ingramcontent.com/pod-product-compliance
Lightning Source LLC
Chambersburg PA
CBHW040310240426
43666CB00021B/2919